AI READINESS

A collaborative design toolkit
for professional services firms

This book is an output of the Innovating Next Generation Services through Collaborative Design (ES/S010475/1) project funded by UK Research and Innovation.

ISBN 978-1-80049-498-5

Copyright © 2021 Oxford Brookes University

Designed and typeset by SomeBrightSpark
www.somespark.co.uk

Copy-edited by Ezri Carlebach

This work is licensed under a Creative Commons Attribution-ShareAlike 4.0 International License.

How to cite this toolkit:
Lucy Kimbell, Ezri Carlebach, Hilary Smyth-Allen, Cristian Gherhes, Makayla Lewis, and Tim Vorley (2021). AI Readiness: A collaborative design toolkit for professional services firms. Oxford Brookes University, Oxford; Practice Management International LLP, Little Berkhamsted.

Co-Publishers

Oxford Brookes is one of the UK's leading modern universities, and is the only UK institution ranked in the top 50 globally for universities under 50 years old. Set in a world-famous student city, it enjoys an international reputation for teaching excellence as well as strong links with business, industry and the public sector.

www.brookes.ac.uk

Supporting the growth, productivity and prosperity of professional services

Driven by a constant search for value and efficiency, the growing use of new technologies, and profound permanent changes in work patterns, most leadership teams are re-evaluating their firm's purpose, strategies, processes and business models. The Forum brings together leadership teams to share ideas on strategic leadership and management excellence, and also acts as their independent voice to policymakers. Our members tell us that we create value by improving their firms, people and clients, and helping them prepare for a post Covid world.

https://www.mpfglobal.com/

> The design sprint methodology set out in the AI Readiness toolkit allowed us to successfully convene a large range of stakeholders to explore the vast opportunities available to the sector through the more effective application of AI and data.

Victoria Purtill
Director of Authorisation and Supervision
Cilex Regulation

> Whether your AI strategy is already well-developed or completely embryonic, the materials and methodology in the AI Readiness toolkit will stimulate really useful discussion and quickly demonstrate that there is more to think about than you ever realised.

Dave Bloor
Chief Technology Officer
Foot Anstey

> Professionals, and especially the 'next generation' leaders, will find the toolkit thought-provoking, challenging and valuable.

Chris Bull
Executive Board Member
GL Law

> The scenarios in the toolkit informed our strategic planning and expanded our horizons, challenging the way we thought about the future.

Louise Thomas
Head of Transformation and Project Management
Burges Salmon LLP

> The AI Readiness toolkit introduction to scenario modelling is a must for any law firm (or indeed any professional services firm) that intends to take AI seriously – and, let's face it, that should be every firm.

Tony Randle
Partner
Shoosmiths

> As a Chartered Accountant I found the AI toolkit to provide practical steps for professional services firms to allow them to asses and introduce technologies that can deliver real value to the client and the practice.

Bob Booth
Cognitive Process Reengineering Lead, UKI
IBM

> The methodologies in the AI Readiness toolkit are extremely useful in shaping and testing innovation strategies.

Stuart Whittle
Director of Business Services and Innovation
Weightmans LLP

> This book provides a structured approach for accountants and other professionals looking to to get ahead in terms of their AI readiness.

Becky Shields
Partner
Moore Kingston Smith LLP

> The toolkit explores options for using AI combining a great mix of academic and practical insight.

Charlotta Cederqvist
Head of Business Development
Law Society of Scotland

Contents

	Foreword		11
1.	**Addressing an urgent need**		
1.1	Introduction		14
1.2	Why this toolkit matters		17
1.3	Who the toolkit is for		18
1.4	When to use the toolkit		20
1.5	How to use the toolkit		23
	1.5.1	Following the AI readiness collaborative design toolkit journey	24
	1.5.2	Using the toolkit to achieve your business goals	26
1.6	Main concepts used in this toolkit		28
	1.6.1	Artificial intelligence (AI)	28
	1.6.2	Business models and business model innovation	32
	1.6.3	Design and the design sprint method	36

2.	**Exploring AI and your firm through the collaborative design sprint**		
2.1	How to organise a design sprint		41
2.2	Remote, in-person or hybrid?		43
2.3	Who to involve in your design sprint		44
2.4	Sample agendas		46
	2.4.1	Agenda 1: One-day design sprint	46
	2.4.2	Agenda 2: Multi-day design sprint	46
2.5	Methods, tools and templates		50
	M0	Define a sprintable challenge	52
	M1	Icebreaker	57
	M2	Understand your business model	59
	M3	Learning from practice	60
	M4	Explore future scenarios	62
	M5	Bring the future firm to life	71
	M6	Explore ai opportunities	73
	M7	Start the innovation roadmap	74
	M8	Define the innovation beneficiaries	80
	M9	Rapid idea generation	84
	M10	Make and review models and mock-ups	87
	M11	Storyboarding	90
	M12	Get 360-degree feedback	93
	M13	Complete the innovation roadmap	94
	M14	Make presentations and share feedback	96
	M15	So what? Now what?	99
	M16	Reflective conversation	101

3. Understanding the landscape

3.1	**What's going on in the landscape for mid-size law and accounting firms**	104
3.2	**Opportunities and challenges of AI readiness**	107
	3.2.1 Opportunities for AI readiness in law and accounting	109
	3.2.2 Challenges of AI readiness in law and accounting	110
3.3	**Learning from practice**	113
3.4	**Current uses of AI in accounting and law firms in England**	115
	3.4.1 Case 1: The accounting or law firm as software vendor	116
	3.4.2 Case 2: The accounting or law firm as data analyser	118
	3.4.3 Case 3: The accounting or law firm as process and project consultant	120
	3.4.4 Case 4: The accounting or law firm as automated business	122
	3.4.5 Case 5: The efficient law or accounting firm	124
	3.4.6 Case 6: The (re)integrated law or accounting firm – capturing value	126
	3.4.7 Case 7: The accounting or law firm as innovation lab	128
3.5	**Approaches to the deployment of AI in accounting and law firms in England**	130
	3.5.1 Approach 1: Addressing the AI competency challenge	131
	3.5.2 Approach 2: The adoption dilemma	132
	3.5.3 Approach 3: Managing expectations	135
	3.5.4 Approach 4: Who needs to use AI in the next generation professional services firm?	136
	3.5.5 Approach 5: Managing the change to the professional career path	138
	3.5.6 Approach 6: Organising digital and data driven professional services	141

4. Exploring futures for professional service firms

4.1	**Introducing scenarios and scenario planning**	146
	4.1.1 Why use scenarios?	147
	4.1.2 How we developed these scenarios	148
4.2	**Overview of the 2030 scenarios**	150
	4.2.1 Using scenarios to convert insights into action	150
	4.2.2 Using scenarios to help with organisational learning	152
	4.2.3 Building an anticipatory capacity in the firm	152
4.3	**Three scenarios for 2030**	154
	4.3.1 Scenario comparison table	156
4.4	**Scenario 1: Platform domination**	158
4.5	**Scenario 2: Bumpy superhighway**	162
4.6	**Scenario 3: Value kaleidoscope**	168

Afterword 175

References, credits & acknowledgements

References	178
Credits & acknowledgements	183

Foreword

Foreword by Stephen Browning

It is now something of a truism to observe that artificial intelligence (AI) and data driven technologies are transforming the global economy. This applies to the UK's services sectors, including the accounting and law firms for whom this toolkit has primarily been developed, as much as any others. There are of course technical challenges to be addressed in the adoption of AI and related technologies, but there are issues of human attitudes and behaviours that are equally – if not more – important. In light of these issues there is considerable value in the multi-disciplinary approach taken to the research and production of this toolkit, covering as it does the technical and organisational challenges, business implications and demands for innovation that confront professional services firms today.

At UK Research & Innovation (UKRI), the UK's largest public funder of Research and Innovation, we have allocated £20m of funding to projects exploring how new technologies could transform the UK's accountancy, insurance and legal services. The Next Generation Services challenge aims to advance technologies such as artificial intelligence and data analytics that can help these services become more efficient and productive and retain their globally competitive position. A central theme of this challenge is the importance of addressing AI readiness among mid-tier accounting and law firms. As technological advancements reshape the professional services sector, it is crucial that these small to medium sized firms are able not only to keep up with developments, but also to stay one step ahead wherever possible. It is UKRI's aim to ensure these firms are primed for a future of positive and sustainable innovation, and we are working with businesses across legal services, accountancy and insurance to build their AI capability, and with technology providers to improve the explainability of their products. This toolkit provides an authoritative review of the current landscape for mid-tier accounting and law firms in England, a powerful lens through which to view the future of professional services firms – both as sites of specific expertise and as businesses – and a unique set of collaborative design tools founded on robust design practice and tested with representative firms from around the UK.

Despite some of the more apocalyptic headlines it is unlikely that AI adoption will lead to mass redundancies in professional services. Instead, AI and related technologies can enhance routine and data-intensive tasks, allowing professionals more time to focus on other, more value-adding activities. There will always be a need for the human understanding and human decision-making that characterise those higher-value tasks, whatever advances technology might make. Our task at UKRI is to help the UK's professional services sector understand the real potential of AI, explore where best to implement it and be ready for the consequences. *AI Readiness: A collaborative design toolkit for professional services firms* offers a significant step in that direction.

Stephen Browning is Next Generation Services challenge director at UK Research & Innovation

1 Addressing an urgent need

1. Addressing an urgent need

1.1	**Introduction**	**14**
1.2	**Why this toolkit matters**	**17**
1.3	**Who the toolkit is for**	**18**
1.4	**When to use the toolkit**	**20**
1.5	**How to use the toolkit**	**23**
	1.5.1 Following the AI readiness collaborative design toolkit journey	**24**
	1.5.2 Using the toolkit to achieve your business goals	**26**
1.6	**Main concepts used in this toolkit**	**28**
	1.6.1 Artificial intelligence (AI)	**28**
	1.6.2 Business models and business model innovation	**32**
	1.6.3 Design and the design sprint method	**36**

1.1 Introduction

The services sector as a whole represents almost 80 per cent of the UK economy, providing more than four million jobs. While contributing 11 per cent to UK productivity, professional services firms face an unprecedented challenge from the rapid spread of artificial intelligence (AI) technologies. AI already "shapes the economic competitiveness of nations and alters how trillions of dollars pulse through global markets".[1] It is a significant driver of enhanced competitiveness and productivity in the UK economy and, spurred by a combination of increasing computer power, unprecedented quantities of data and rapidly evolving machine learning, is poised to transform the way professional services firms do business and disrupt many long-established practices. Amidst continued technological advancement and increased international competition, and with new competitors already capitalising on AI's potential, there is now an urgent need for established professional services firms to consider both the risks and the opportunities AI brings.

However, these potential opportunities have not been widely embraced. This is partly due to the challenges to established business models, talent strategies and data management; and partly because the sector continues to experience increasing profitability year on year. And while professional bodies such as ICAEW[2] and The Law Society[3] have paid close attention to AI's strategic and operational impact, approaches within the sector have become polarised. At one end of the spectrum the Big Four and Magic Circle firms have invested heavily to get ahead of the game, while at the other end a growing number of start-ups threatens to disrupt established firms. Although an important proportion of the overall sector, mid-tier firms are too small individually to make a comprehensive investment in new technologies, yet the consequences of failing to do so are too big to ignore. Therefore, this toolkit has been created to support mid-tier firms at risk from these developments, helping them prepare for future competitiveness.

Before professional services firms can embark on the process of procuring and implementing AI and other advanced digital solutions, they need to think about what this means for their day-to-day working reality. While the promise of such technologies has proved a lure for many organisations, AI is not a technology that can simply be plugged into existing systems and utilised without any change to organisational practices. This disruptive potential means professional services firms must carefully think through the implications of AI for the way they operate. There will be consequences for their business models, differential impact on employees across the organisation, and a need to reimagine how they function as organisations. It can be helpful to think of it as a journey that firms must undertake if they are to maximise the opportunities AI presents.

The first steps on this journey are concerned with gaining what is known as 'AI readiness'. Thus, a central aim of this toolkit is to advance the AI readiness of professional services firms. The toolkit explains how to work through a series of tested and proven activities that challenge conventional understanding of the way professional services firms operate as businesses. In doing so, firms will be better able to respond to the challenges of AI readiness by considering plausible future scenarios, identifying opportunities for business model innovation and planning for the necessary changes.

Although this toolkit will have applications beyond mid-tier professional services firms, we are throughout addressing leaders, innovators and, indeed, everyone working in such firms. Whether you are just starting to consider how AI might benefit your firm, or have already identified areas of opportunity, this toolkit can help. It will guide you on your AI readiness journey, provide knowledge and resources to help you explore the wider issues and show you how to use a specially adapted version of the design sprint methodology. Professional services firms like yours are critical to the UK economy and - beyond the GDP and labour market statistics - to civil society, families and individuals. Since work began on this toolkit, the trauma and disruption wrought by the global COVID-19 pandemic added further complexity to the process of AI readiness. If anything, the urgency now is greater than ever. No single product or process can bring about the level of innovation that is needed in every firm where such innovation will make a difference. Nevertheless, we hope this toolkit proves to be a practical resource for your specific AI-related and wider business innovation needs.

1 Buchanan (2020).

2 ICAEW (2018).

3 Law Society (2018a).

Artificial intelligence (AI) has the potential to transform the way professional services firms do business and will disrupt many long-established practices.

AI Readiness

1.2

Image: Thirdman on Pexels

1.2 **Why this toolkit matters**

Given the potential impact of AI on every aspect of human affairs it is not surprising to find frequent references to a 'tsunami' of AI-driven innovation sweeping the professions and almost every other business sector. Yet innovation has tended to be considered a low priority by professional services firms,[4] leading to a general resistance to the potential of new technologies to change traditional business practices.[5] Research on the future of the professions highlights the challenges they face in thinking about the future, the fundamental problems regarding the way in which they are organised and the potential of new technologies to impact current working practices.[6] While new technologies can drive efficiency and productivity in accounting and law firms, especially by leveraging the potential of data,[7] they also reduce the need for human labour in areas such as volume and transactional work, meaning firms need to be agile and ready to adapt.

AI has particular potential for transformative change in professional services. In legal services, AI can radically alter the production and consumption of law and even the nature of law itself.[8] This may allow for greater efficiency, openness, transparency and personalisation of services, but also creates challenges to trust between clients and lawyers, changes to the broader regulatory environment and, potentially, the replacement of human lawyers entirely.[9] However, just as electricity only led to significant productivity improvements in manufacturing after the restructuring of systems, logistics and labour roles, so the benefits of AI may require a complete rethinking of accounting and legal services provision. Therefore, the transformative nature of AI-enabled technologies presents challenges as well as opportunities for incumbents, not least because AI continues to develop rapidly and to permeate domains of activity in professional services and beyond. It is thus critical to consider how AI may transform the business and the practice of professional services firms in the short term, along with the implications for the future of professional services as a whole. The implementation of AI is not as straightforward as other technologies which can be plugged into business operations without much disruption. Capitalising on its opportunities therefore necessitates a transformation of existing practices and ways of doing business. Ultimately, *AI Readiness: A collaborative design toolkit for professional services firms* matters because it guides you through a series of specially designed activities to identify areas where AI can add value to your firm; helps you understand what needs to change within your firm; and builds your knowledge of the barriers to AI readiness and how you might overcome them.

4 LexisNexis (2014); Brooks et al. (2018a).
5 Ribstein (2010).
6 Susskind and Susskind (2015).
7 Slaughter and May (2017).
8 Brooks et al. (2020).
9 Rostain (2017); Greenleaf et al. (2018).

1.3 **Who the toolkit is for**

The AI readiness toolkit is for individuals and teams within professional services firms who have a remit for innovation and technology adoption, or who simply want to support AI readiness in their firm and explore the options in an innovative way. This includes, but is not limited to, senior and managing partners, fee-earners, innovation teams, innovation group leads, IT architects, legal engineers, trainees and support executive. While this toolkit has been designed specifically for professional services firms, a comparable mix of people would be needed in any type of organisation. The research undertaken and the experience of collaborative design amassed in the process of creating this toolkit show that the more diverse the team working on an AI solution, the more comprehensive and realistic the roadmap to its implementation.

Exploring the possibilities for AI within your firm may start with a small team of technology specialists and senior leaders identifying potential use-cases and assessing the appropriateness of existing technologies. But sourcing AI solutions and developing a comprehensive approach to their implementation is best done with multiple perspectives from across the organisation. The rationale for this approach lies in the fact that AI is likely to impact all aspects of service delivery, and thus affects the roles of everyone involved. In putting together a team to make best use of this toolkit it is important to decide who you would like to involve, who you need to involve, and whose involvement is critical for developing viable solutions.

We worked with a range of UK professional services firms to create this toolkit. In some cases, we were invited to run sessions by partners or senior fee-earners, while in others we worked with senior persons responsible for developing and delivering the firm's technology or innovation strategy; often in fact, the same person. Based on these interactions, we suggest the following will be needed to translate the toolkit's insights into concrete actions:

- If there is no AI strategy in place, the involvement of a senior partner, or the managing partner, to create space for exploring the potential of AI. If there is a strategy, and in addition to senior leadership, the involvement of the person responsible for its development and implementation.
- The involvement of people from different parts of the business whose roles might be changed or challenged by AI, including service delivery and business support functions such as operations, technology, talent management, risk management and marketing and communications.

This toolkit is based on research examining the experiences and challenges of UK professional services firms in using AI. Using design thinking and scenarios, the toolkit has been piloted with a range of legal and accounting firms to improve their AI readiness.

Image: Alesia Kazantceva on Unsplash

1.4 When to use the toolkit

Firms in the professional services sector are at different stages of AI readiness. While some are just starting to think about the possibilities of AI, others have identified solutions but need to consider the implications for business models. This toolkit supports all stages in the journey, from providing the basis for a discussion of the possibilities all the way through to supporting the development of a comprehensive roadmap for AI implementation. Based on the stage at which your firm finds itself, you may wish to consider AI readiness in relation to the following scenarios:

1. Thinking about the possibilities of AI
At the initial stage of the AI readiness journey, you will likely be exploring the implications and opportunities of AI for your firm. This may involve technology specialists and senior leaders looking at how AI could benefit your business and your clients.

2. Thinking about what AI means for you as a business
You are considering the introduction of AI as a viable option and exploring possible vendor solutions, or the potential to develop solutions in-house.

3. Thinking about AI beyond the technology
You have already identified solutions, or considered in-house development, and are now thinking about the wider implications of AI readiness for your firm. This may involve the opportunity to create efficiencies and develop new AI-enabled specialisations. However, you realise that implementing AI solutions is not straightforward and that you need to consider the implications for your business model; specifically, how this will affect the delivery of your service, who will be impacted and what that might look like, and how your value proposition may change as a result.

4. Thinking about specific opportunities and looking to design and deliver AI solutions
At this stage, you have a good understanding of AI technologies, have identified desirable solutions and are aware of the implications for your business model. You are ready to consider the specific opportunities and risks of adopting a particular AI technology.

Connecting AI readiness to business goals

When considering AI readiness, it is important to focus on specific problems that you want to solve, or opportunities you want to address, to connect your technology and innovation strategy to business goals. This is because existing AI technologies are narrow, and hence specific in what they can achieve for particular organisational areas or tasks. While AI can address various issues and opportunities within an organisation, each will be particular to your situation, your stage in the AI readiness journey and your business goals. Whether you are just starting to think about the possibilities of AI, or you are ready to work on specific AI solutions, the following options can help focus your efforts:

1. Focus on professional practice
For example, if you are a legal services firm you may want to explore AI technologies that automate repetitive tasks, such as NDA review, legal research and contract review.

2. Focus on the business
This relates to aspects of service delivery such as workflow automation, time keeping, eBilling, contract management and general speed of processing.

3. Reducing inefficiencies
This involves a focus on cutting waste and increasing productivity and may include a combination of AI technologies to improve both your practice and your service delivery.

4. New charging and costing models
This involves rethinking your economic model. It is already evident that AI technologies can create efficiencies that significantly reduce the time required to complete a task, often from hours to minutes or seconds.[10] Using this toolkit will help you consider the challenges to your current economic model, in particular how you charge for your services and how this may need to change.

10 See Alarie et al. (2018).

Image: Christopher Burns on Unsplash

Image: Ahmad Dirini on Unsplash

1.5 AI Readiness

1.5 How to use the toolkit

The toolkit consists of a set of 17 methods, some of which include specially designed tools and templates; a guided design sprint journey process; and a set of reports that explore the AI readiness ecosystem for professional services firms, as it exists now and in three detailed future scenarios. We have illustrated a suggested path for the journey of discovery that toolkit users can take. We will say more about the methods, tools and templates in the next section of the toolkit. In the meantime, you can familiarise yourself with the milestones of the journey as depicted in the illustration on pages 24 and 25.

The journey is divided into four phases: **examine \ explore \ develop \ reflect.** There are 11 steps all together, and each step offers you a series of questions to consider; directs you to the related method or methods in the toolkit; and identifies optimal points at which to engage with the detailed reports provided. This represents a logical sequence derived from the toolkit production team's knowledge and expertise and enhanced by the insights of senior staff from professional services firms who have taken part in test workshops. Nevertheless, we would encourage you to play around with the elements and dip in and out of the reports to get to know the environment within which the toolkit operates, and to get a feel for what might work in your specific situation.

The toolkit in numbers

17 Seventeen collaborative **design** methods

11 Eleven **discovery** journey steps

7 Seven **cases** of current uses of AI in accounting and law firms in England

6 Six **approaches** to the deployment of AI in accounting and law firms in England

3 Three future **scenarios** for professional services firms in 2030

1.5.1 Following the AI Readiness collaborative design toolkit journey

Start / Repeat

Phase 1: Examine

Step 1
Understand the context

- What does AI mean for you, your business and your professional practice?
- Why is this important now?
- How can collaborative design methods help?

Read the toolkit section 'Addressing an urgent need'

M0 Define a Sprintable Challenge
Generates a written definition of the challenge

M1 Icebreaker
Generates openness and connections among participants

Step 2
Understand your business model

- How does your business create value now?
- Who benefits from that?
- What does it look like when you map it visually?

M2 Understand your business model
Generates a completed Business Model Template

Step 3
Learning from practice: Current uses of AI and approaches to AI adoption

- Which examples from the research are most relevant to you?
- What could your firm achieve using AI?
- Which tasks would best be AI enabled/augmented?
- What might the consequences look like for your firm and your clients?

Read the toolkit section 'Understanding the landscape'

M3 Learning from practice
Generates a completed Business Model Template

Step 5
Explore AI opportunities

- Which AI opportunity is most relevant to your firm?
- How does it impact your business model?
- What are the business outcomes?
- Is it just about process automation or can this opportunity impact professional expertise?
- What direction does your Innovation Roadmap suggest you take?

M7 Start the Innovation Roadmap
Generates a partially-completed Innovation Roadmap

M6 Explore AI opportunities
Select from one of a set of potential AI opportunities for your firm

Step 4
Explore future scenarios

- What might the future be like for professional services?
- What aspects of these possible futures will impact your firm?
- How would your firm's current strategy perform in each future scenario?
- What will people in the future say about your choices today?

M5 Bring the firm's future to life
Generates mock-ups of media/social media reports from the future

M4 Explore future scenarios
Generates insights into the strategic implications of future scenarios

Read the toolkit section 'Exploring futures for professional services firms.'

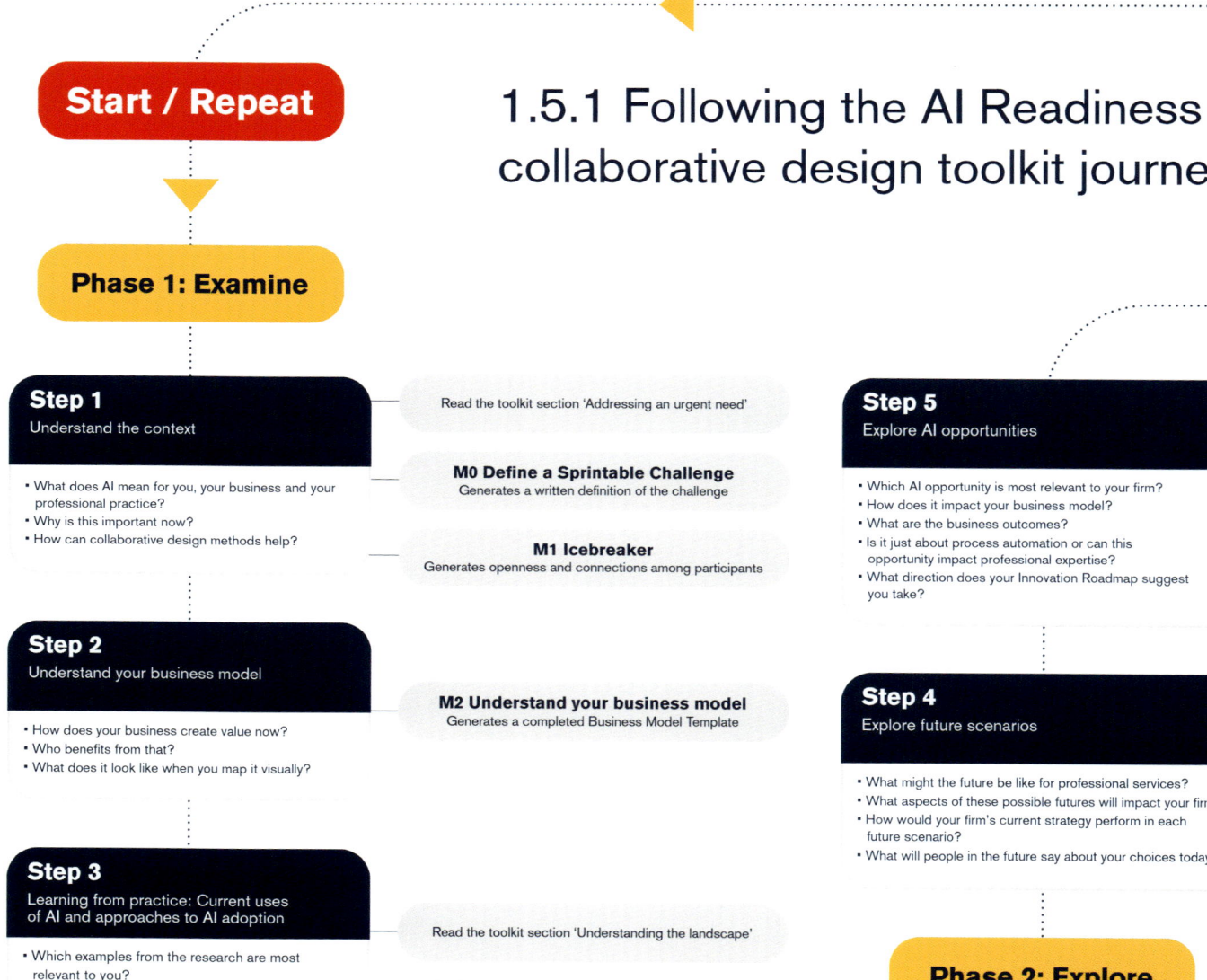

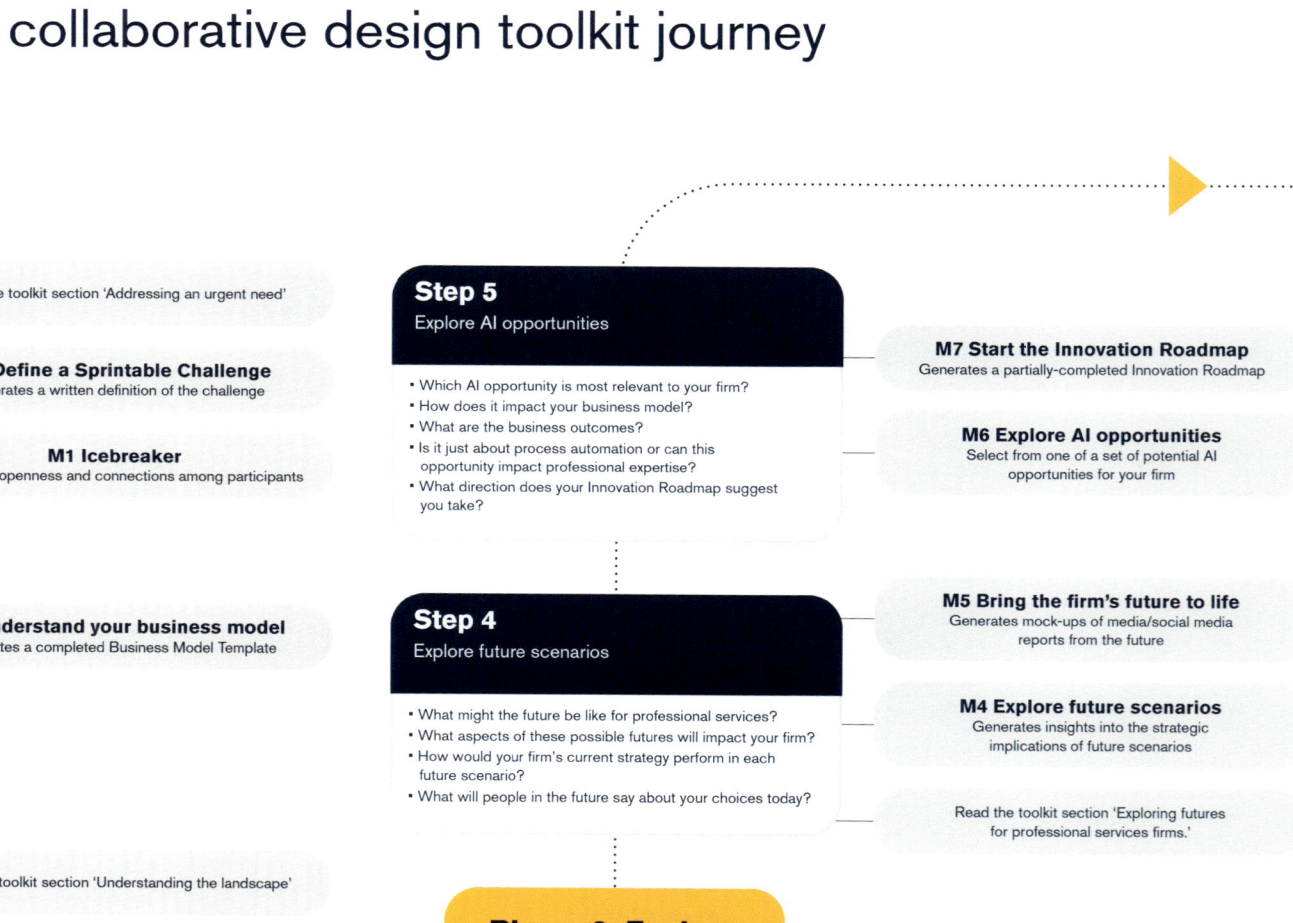

Phase 2: Explore

Step 11
The context has now changed

- Because of what you created in the sprint
- Because of other internal factors
- Because of external factors
• What is the new opportunity for a collaborative design sprint?

Revisit M0 Define a Sprintable Challenge

Step 10
Reflect on the process and discuss the implications

• How can you take this further?
• What will you tell the Managing Partner?
• What does it mean for your role and for careers in your firm?
• How will the profession change overall?

M16 Reflective conversation
Gives colleagues a chance to explore the consequences of everything they've done on the sprint journey

Phase 3: Develop

M8 Define the innovation beneficiaries
Generates a set of recognisable but flexible personas relevant to your firm and sector

Step 6
Design the AI-enabled firm or service

M9 Rapid idea generation
Generates a broad range of ideas created by participants

Step 9*
Ask 'So what? Now what?'

• What insights have you gained?
• What difference will this make?
• What happens next?
• What might be the consequence of not acting?

*It can be helpful to run a 'mini' version of this exercise after some or all of the preceding steps.

M15 So What? Now What?
Generates agreement on the experience and relevance of the sprint process and builds commitment to action

• Who are the beneficiaries of the innovation?
• How would they benefit?
• How would other firms approach creating that benefit?
• What would the future AI-enabled firm or service look like?
• What would the future AI-enabled user/client journey look like?

M10 Make & review models & mock-ups
Generates a set of models and mock-ups from recyclable materials

M11 Storyboarding
Generates a set of stories in a visually engaging format

Step 8
Presentations and feedback

Step 7
Refine your innovation

M12 Get 360-degree feedback
Generates peer insights to revise innovation concepts

• What is the challenge or opportunity in terms of the business model?
• What AI capability do you want to use?
• What business model innovation does this suggest or require?
• What might be the related outcome(s)?
• What would have to change?
• What are the potential barriers?

M14 Presentations and feedback
Gives colleagues a chance to explain their ideas and get feedback from key stakeholders

• Which of the approaches described in the research is most relevant to your firm or idea?
• If you invested in your future idea, what would have to change?
• What is the risk in making that change and what would mitigate the risk?
• Who would you have to engage with or persuade?

M13 Complete the Innovation Roadmap
Generates a completed Innovation Roadmap

Phase 4: Reflect

1.5.2 Using the toolkit to achieve your business goals

Having walked through the steps of the design sprint in the illustration in 1.5.1 above, you may find it useful to review the example use cases, both for the design sprint method as a whole and for some of its constituent parts, presented below. They offer pointers to relevant resources to work with and possible actions to take, either on your own or with colleagues (possibly, but not necessarily, in a dedicated sprint team), whether you wish to examine, explore, design and/or lead aspects of the AI readiness journey in your firm.

The sequence can be followed consecutively if you intend to complete the whole sprint. For example, the **lead** use case requires the completion of all design sprint activities included in **examine, explore** and **design,** while firms that just want to **explore** need only go through the activities in **examine** and **explore.** Organising the toolkit in this way ensures there is a flow and makes it easier for you to break down your approach over several days or weeks, if you're unable to do it all in one day or one week. In the latter case, week one might be devoted to reading the background information, week two may be used for exploring future scenarios, and so on, until you have completed all the activities.

If you decide to use the toolkit to run a full design sprint, it would be advisable to begin with the first tool, **M0** Define a sprintable challenge. However, it may not be a necessary first step for other ways of using this toolkit, for example if you are only looking to familiarise yourself with the main concepts or explore the potential of different AI-enabled technologies for your firm. The toolkit's modular structure makes it more accessible and flexible, so you can quickly benefit from using it whether you are interested in starting with limited experimentation or want to take the plunge and complete a sprint straight away. The toolkit has also been designed for repeated use, such as exploring different AI-enabled technologies or addressing other, non-AI related sprintable challenges (which is why step 11 appears at the end of the journey). Repeated use compounds the benefits, since you and your colleagues will become familiar with the collaborative design methodology and can focus on solution development.

	1. Read these toolkit sections	2. Use these methods to turn insights to action
I/We want to examine... ...what's going on in the landscape of AI in professional services firms	'Understanding the Landscape'	Use **M3** Learning from Practice
...business models and business model innovation in professional services firms	'Main concepts used in this toolkit"	Use **M2** Understand Your Business Model Use **M6** Explore Innovation Opportunitites
...how professional services firms are using AI	'Current uses of AI in accounting and law firms in England'	Use **M3** Learning from Practice
...approaches professional services firms are taking to implement AI solutions	'Approaches to the deployment of AI in accounting and law firms in England'	Use **M7** Start the Innovation Roadmap Use **M13** Complete the Innovation Roadmap
I/We want to explore... ...potential future scenarios for professional services firms	'Exploring futures for professional services firms'	
...our current business model		Use **M2** Understand Your Business Model
...how AI could change our business model		Use **M6** Explore Innovation Opportunities
...our current business (or AI or technology) strategy in different future scenariosour business model	'Three scenarios for 2030'	Use **M4** Explore Future Scenarios
I/We want to develop... ...a shared understanding of future uncertainties around AI for professional services	'Three scenarios for 2030'	Use **M4** Explore Future Scenarios Use **M5** Bring the Future Firm to Life
...a shared vision for AI in our firm, with how we might become more AI ready		Use **M6** to **M15**
...a better understanding of how what being AI ready might mean for our firm	'Approaches to the deployment of AI in accounting and law firms in England'	Use **M6** to **M15**
I/We want to lead... ...a process that allows our firm to develop a better understanding		Use **M0** Define a sprintable challenge Use the sample agendas to design your own sprint
...the development of an innovation capability in our firm	'Design and the design sprint method'	Focus on methods **M6** to **M14**

1.6 Main concepts used in this toolkit

1.6.1 Artificial intelligence (AI)

The term 'artificial intelligence' was coined in 1955 by computer scientist John McCarthy to describe "the science and engineering of making intelligent machines, especially intelligent computer programs".[11] However, despite being around for more than six decades, AI remains "a notoriously difficult term to define",[12] even if, somewhat ironically, "the lack of a precise, universally accepted definition of AI probably has helped the field to grow".[13] Since AI is concerned with studying and developing systems - whether of computers or more general machines - that act rationally (i.e., that are intelligent agents), the main goal of such systems is to take the best possible actions in a given situation. For example, an AI chess system acts rationally if it makes the best possible moves to win a game given the current chess board positions. While the exact meaning of 'intelligent' in this context is still up for debate, these definitions offer at least an outline of the functions AI-enabled technologies should perform in order to be classified as such; that is, tasks normally requiring human intelligence.

AI is often referred to as a general-purpose technology because of its potential uses across different sectors, the new opportunities it opens up and its rapid development in recent years.[14] Current AI applications fall into two categories, 'narrow' and 'general'. Narrow applications refer to technologies developed for carrying out specifically prescribed tasks using machine learning. These include statistically analysing large, historical data sets[15] to carry out tasks such as face and speech recognition, which would normally require human intelligence. While these applications still only perform a limited range of tasks, they have seen significant progress in recent years. On the other hand, little or no progress has been made in developing artificial general intelligence.[16] This remains an important endeavour for computer scientists, albeit one with remote prospects.

AI is often conflated with machine learning, which is a subfield of artificial intelligence. Machine learning is defined as the ability of a computer to learn to perform a task without being explicitly programmed to do so. The fuzziness around what AI actually is has led to confusion about what represents 'true AI' in different applications. Many software products labelled as 'AI' do not perform functions generally understood as AI. Research on the challenges of transformation in legal services has highlighted that automation, rather than 'true AI' capability, underpins the majority of new technologies.[17] Therefore, before engaging in AI readiness and considering potential solutions it is important to understand the types of AI-enabled technologies found in the professional services sector and their areas of applicability. While many of the new technologies permeating professional services are underpinned by automation rather than 'true AI', they can be seen as stepping-stones towards the latter. Understanding the potential of these technologies and exploring where they can add value in your organisation will enable you to become AI-ready.

11 McCarthy (2007) p. 2.
12 Alarie et al. (2018) p.115.
13 Stone et al. (2016).
14 Agrawal et al. (2019).
15 Spiegelhalter (2019).
16 House of Lords (2018).
17 Brooks et al. (2020).

Image: Fabio Ballasina on Unsplash

Ethical problems and legal uncertainties

There is a great deal of debate concerning ethical issues raised by AI's development and use. It is now well understood, for instance, that machine learning and other software tend to reproduce many structural inequalities. The consequences in the real world can be very damaging, such as when police departments develop increasingly powerful mass digital surveillance systems; or when applicant screening software reproduces historical biases in a company's hiring processes. Ethical issues involving AI range from data privacy and the gig economy to copyright and intellectual property disputes, but also extend far beyond the well-known examples. The various forms that algorithms take, and their insertion into every aspect of public life, are now "generating the bounded conditions of what a democracy, a border crossing, a social movement, an election, or a public protest could be" and algorithms have thus become "ethicopolitical beings in the world".[18] AI is also seen as enabling the "instrumentalization of data... for the purposes of a highly intentional program of manipulation and behavioral modification".[19]

While arguments of this nature prioritise the risk to human rights - even, potentially, to legible personhood under algorithmic outputs - others explore how AI shifts corporate accountability. When an organisation deploys an automated decision-making system, such as a resumé scanner, who should be held responsible for any bias in that software? The company using the technology? The company who developed or sold the technology? Any contractors who contributed to its programming? If there is a 'human-in-the-loop' in a technologically-assisted decision-making procedure, how does that change the answers to these questions, if at all? Others are exploring the emergence of rights and responsibilities attaching to AI; "If AI were to cause harm, or to create something beneficial, who should be held responsible? Are there moral or pragmatic grounds for granting AI legal protections and responsibilities?"[20] At present it would appear that courts will not entertain the prospect of AI gaining such protections. In a case in Singapore concerning losses sustained by the client of a company offering an AI-based crypto-currency trading system, the Singapore International Commercial Court concluded that algorithms "have no mind of their own. They operate when called upon to do so in a pre-ordained manner".[21]

Image: Fabio Ballasina on Unsplash

Meanwhile, exaggerated visions of AI have captured the public imagination. Much of the public discourse about AI, and even substantial discussion among AI ethicists, concerns hypothetical and relatively unlikely potential futures of existential threats to humanity and meaningfully self-conscious robots.

It will require significant efforts on the part of governments, civil society, judicial institutions and (human) experts to understand, track and act on the ethical and legal questions of substantial concern posed by AI and translate these into regulation and compliance. These questions and needs should remain visible in every organisation's AI readiness journey.

The practice of professional services vs the business of professional services

In becoming AI ready it is important to understand the purpose or function for which you intend to use AI. There is a distinction between AI application in the practice of professional services and in the business of professional services. Both offer opportunities for improving productivity and competitiveness, although the former is ultimately more likely to shape the future of the professions. Arguably, the client's experience of professional services is determined by the combination of the service provider's practice and business. It is important to recognise that these two aspects cannot be entirely separated.

The practice of professional services firms

Legal and accounting firms are knowledge-intensive and rely on professional expertise to deliver their services. However, there is a growing demand for provision of high-quality services in conjunction with fee certainty. This has led law and accounting firms to extend the scope of their services, so that they not only analyse legal and accounting matters, but also provide clients with business advice and tools, including new technology. This has created an expectation that legal and accounting professionals will expand their roles and, for example, gain skills such as data handling and analysis. AI has proven its worth in aiding professionals with this aspect of their changing work requirements. Firms must not only think about how technology can be used to analyse data effectively (which has also led to the emergence of new professional roles), but also deliver a better technological method for managing projects to ensure workflows are followed and effective services provided. This depends on firms examining their own process efficiencies, as well as those of their clients. At the same time, automating aspects of law and accounting can help firms achieve process and cost efficiencies. Accountants and lawyers have traditionally enjoyed considerable autonomy in the organisation of their work. However, in the face of increasing client demand for cost reduction, cost predictability and improved efficiency, technology allows firms to explore the potential of fixed-price service offering and has incentivised them to adopt new ways of providing services. The efficient professional services firm uses software capabilities and associated task redesign to make significant reductions to the amount of time and cost needed in repetitive, high-volume areas such as document review. We therefore refer to the role of AI in professional services practice to describe where AI technologies are used to augment and improve the practice of the professions. This may include the use of AI technologies to automate more labour-intensive activities where little professional judgement is required, increasing the accuracy of activities involved in professional practice and improving the basis upon which professionals make judgements. The opportunity in employing AI is thus to promote higher value, higher quality professional services practice.

The business of professional services firms

The use of AI technologies in the business of professional services is most commonly associated with business process management and workflow. There is an overlap here with the wider digital transformation of firms, which is enabling them to operate in more agile ways by streamlining processes. Such practices are understood as necessary in fast-moving business environments and have aspects that are internal (employee) facing and external (client) facing. The scope also ranges across the business, from IT and Communications to HR and Finance. The business of professional services therefore refers to using technology to identify and automate repetitive tasks, enhance transparency, streamline business processes, productise routine functions and shorten delivery cycles.[22]

18 Amoore (2020).
19 Zuboff (2019).
20 Turner (2019).
21 B2C2 v Quoine (2019).
22 Cohen (2018).

1.6.2 Business models and business model innovation

A central component of this toolkit is its focus on business models in relation to AI readiness. The toolkit is designed to help you understand your current business model as well as to challenge your understanding of innovation. Using the toolkit will prompt you to think about opportunities for business model innovation, because AI readiness is not a straightforward technology adoption process. Rather, it requires you to think about the implications for your business model and how that needs to change or adapt to maximise the intended benefits. Given the transformative potential of AI in professional services, it is critical to explore AI readiness in relation to the business model. Therefore, there are concepts related to business models and business model innovation presented in this toolkit to help you consider the impact and the implications of AI across your business. Integrating these concepts in your firm will be critical to successful AI readiness.

Business models

The various activities utilising the business model concept will challenge your understanding of your firm's current business model and guide you to identify opportunities from AI readiness in different areas of your business. They will also encourage you to consider the implications for the different dimensions of your business model outlined below, the opportunities for business model innovation and the challenges and risks that need to be addressed. Therefore, it is important to first understand what a business model is, as well as what it is not. Firms often confuse their business model with their business plan.[23] While studies have shown that business planning is generally a beneficial and growth-driving activity,[24] a business plan is essentially a document setting out future objectives and strategies for achieving them. The business model, on the other hand, refers to how the company operates to make money. It can be understood as a "blueprint of how a company does business".[25] Importantly, it comprises three functions; how a firm creates, delivers and captures value from its operations.[26]

There are multiple frameworks and approaches that seek to conceptualise the nature of the business model, such as the well-known Business Model Canvas.[27] However, many of these frameworks are static. They don't show how the different functions of the business model interrelate and, importantly, do little to support innovation. We conceptualise the business model in relation to the three functions mentioned above - creating, delivering and capturing value - and divide it into three corresponding dimensions; offering, experience and configuration.

Each of these dimensions comprises further subdimensions relating to different aspects of the business.[28] These are explained below, along with the implications for AI readiness.

23 Brooks et al. (2018b).
24 e.g., Brinckmann et al. (2010); Osiyevskyy et al. (2013).
25 Osterwalder et al. (2005) p. 4.
26 Zott and Amit (2007).
27 Osterwalder et al. (2005).
28 Keeley et al. (2013).

"A good business model answers Peter Drucker's age old questions, 'Who is the customer? And what does the customer value?' It also answers the fundamental questions every manager must ask: How do we make money in this business? What is the underlying economic logic that explains how we can deliver value to customers at an appropriate cost?"[29]

AI Readiness

1.6.2

Image: Arthur Mazi on Unsplash

Offering

The offering refers to the service, or range of services, offered to clients. This is how companies create value for customers and is therefore the main focus of innovation within most companies. A typical question to help understand your offering is, how does your business create value and enhance the performance of your customers? AI solutions in relation to the offering focus on the creation of new, AI-enabled services. Such new services will likely have implications for other aspects of your business, so it is important to consider the experience and configuration dimensions.

Experience

Experience refers to how you engage with your client and how they engage with you. It includes aspects such as brand, interactions and channels, to capture the multiple ways in which your clients experience your service. Typical questions to help you understand this dimension of your business model are: How do your customers interact with your business (physically, digitally or both)? And how does your business build trust with customers? Innovation in experience, prompted by the increasing digitalisation of business, can help your company develop a competitive advantage. AI solutions focusing on this dimension, or with implications for this dimension, will prompt you to consider how the adoption of specific technologies will change the way you and your clients interact and engage with each other.

Configuration

Configuration refers to how your firm is organised not only to create, but also to capture value from its operations. It includes aspects such as the revenue model, network, structure and transactions. Typical questions to help you understand this dimension of your business model are: What transactions does your business have with customers? And how are your skills, capabilities and resources aligned to your revenue model(s)? Innovation in configuration can help your firm leverage its strengths, reduce costs and develop new revenue streams. AI solutions affecting this dimension will prompt you to consider what needs to change in your service delivery structure, as well as how innovation in the configuration of your firm through AI readiness can create competitive advantage.

Business model innovation

AI readiness not only requires you to think about the implications for your business model, but also creates opportunities to gain competitive advantage by innovating in the way you operate, i.e., your business model. A particular challenge is the tendency of most companies to "prefer 'more of the same' (mostly product) innovations", which means that "most companies rarely, if ever, change or even question their business models".[30] But there are other dimensions of the business model that can be innovated, and while new technologies such as AI and machine learning primarily enable product, process or service innovation, focusing efforts solely on the offering provides a truncated view of innovation and limits the opportunity to take advantage of AI. Importantly, business model innovation goes beyond a static, firm-based and supply-side driven approach, also known as the 'inside out' approach, which centres on how internal capabilities can be leveraged to create products and services to offer to the market. Business model innovation adopts an 'outside in' perspective, encouraging a dynamic, market-based and demand-side driven approach that is externally oriented and focused on how best to address evolving customer needs and market trends. As such, business model innovation is about fundamentally rethinking your business around a clear - though not always obvious - customer need, then (re)aligning your resources, processes and revenue model with this new value proposition. Distinct from technological and product innovation, this requires a holistic approach and generates different competitive effects. It involves "the search for new logics of the firm",[31] which redefine how value is created, captured and delivered. Business model innovation often involves making simultaneous, coordinated and internally consistent changes to multiple aspects of the business model to reignite growth, combat disruption, or access new markets.[32]

Business model innovation is about "delivering existing products that are produced by existing technologies to existing markets. And because it often involves changes invisible to the outside world, it can bring advantages that are hard to copy."[33] Adding AI technologies to the mix creates additional opportunities.

30 Taran et al. (2015) p. 302.
31 Casadesus-Masanell and Zhu (2013) p. 464.
32 Brooks et al. (2018a).
33 Girotra and Netessine (2014).

1.6.3 Design and the design sprint method

Design is a broad and diverse professional field and, unlike law and accounting, entry to the profession is not regulated. This results in a huge variety in ways of doing things. Variants include product, communication, fashion and interaction design and there are important overlaps with, and differences to, fields such as engineering, computer science and architecture. Studies of how designers work highlight particular aspects of designing that can be adapted to other disciplines. For example: How they handle uncertainty; maintain a focus on people's experiences of technologies, organisations or policies; use visualisation and materialisation to bring ideas to life and share them; and use small-scale experimentation to advance ideas. As studies of design and its role in innovation have shown, firms that build up this capability have competitive advantages, such as time to market, revenue growth and increased share price.[34] What makes this approach relevant to AI readiness in a professional services firm is the high level of uncertainty about technologies, markets and innovation in the operating environment in which those firms find themselves. One of the reasons for using an approach associated with contemporary design is the emphasis it places on opening up innovation to a broad range of perspectives and on participation in the generating and testing of ideas through workshops, prototyping and reflective conversations. An AI strategy might be written, as a piece of analysis, by a single author, but its execution will require examining the opportunities and implications from multiple angles. Here, a design-based approach serves as a capability for improving the quality of the strategy itself, as well as creating meaningful experiences for those involved in its development.

Design thinking

The approach embedded in this toolkit is based on a methodology that has been popularised over the past decade in business and public sector innovation.[35] Often known as 'design thinking' (or sometimes service design, strategic design or design innovation), this is an approach to exploring issues and opportunities that draws on the professional practices of designers. The popularity of design thinking has led to various descriptions, case studies and toolkits being used to broaden understanding of and access to it.[36] The premise of design thinking is that the ways in which designers go about designing are of value to people such as managers, leaders, entrepreneurs and policy makers who want to develop, test and implement new ideas. Such is the enthusiasm for design and design thinking that elements of this innovation methodology can now be found in all sorts of businesses, learning and development programmes, toolkits and digital collaboration platforms. Many of these developments sprang from both successes and failures in carrying out digital innovation. A company-wide design hackathon at Microsoft resulted in novel solutions to meet the needs of people with disabilities.[37] IBM developed a version of design thinking to better connect its digital capabilities with user needs.[38] And within professional services, firms such as Accenture[39] and EY[40] have developed or acquired expertise in service design and design thinking to augment their skills in data analytics and business consulting.

While 'thinking' is necessarily involved in designing, just as relevant is a set of practices, methods and tools used by contemporary designers, and a culture in which these are embedded. When using the set of approaches collectively known as design thinking, it's important to be aware that they are not neutral. The culture of designers, for example, rewards generating new ideas rather than reviewing what might already be available, opening up issues for exploration rather than finalising things, and zooming in on objects and people's interactions with them rather than analysing the constraining and enabling systems and processes in which they are found. Therefore, when developing this toolkit, we were mindful of both the strengths and weaknesses of this approach, and we have adapted it for the professional services context. Since design thinking has been taken up and championed in sectors from consumer goods and technology systems to policy making and financial services, it's not surprising to find a growing interest in using the approach within professional services.

Design sprinting

Use of the term 'sprint' in business has origins in software development. With the investments in information and communication technologies made in the early 2000s, new ways of working emerged to leverage their potential and avoid some of the long-standing problems associated with software and digital infrastructure projects. The sprint is a method for rapidly identifying ways of speeding up delivery, connecting technological opportunities with user needs and reducing bugs and errors. It also helps to limit the 'scope creep' that was often associated with software development projects, which tended to result in reams of documentation but little usable software. The specific characteristic of a sprint (related terms include 'agile' and 'scrum'[41]) is that it's a time-bounded commitment during which a development team works together to deliver working software. Instead of one giant project, this approach breaks development down into iterative learning cycles with an emphasis on collaboration and delivery.

Although we are using the term 'sprint' for this toolkit, our focus is not on technology development. Rather, we're borrowing the software sprint's emphasis on rapid learning cycles, looking at the implications of technology proposals from multiple perspectives and delivery of outcomes that can be built on. We're following in the footsteps of others who have applied this approach to business problems. For example, a team at Google Ventures developed their own sprint methodology, defining it as "a five-day process for answering critical business questions through design, prototyping, and testing ideas with customers".[42] Global consultancy firm McKinsey has a version called the 'concept sprint', which they see as an innovation process that can "turn an 'idea' into something that has a greater chance of seeing the light of day and succeeding in the marketplace".[43]

There have also been experiments using the approach to develop public policy, for example in the work of the UK government's Policy Lab,[44] healthcare challenges such as cancer research,[45] and a regional approach to carbon-neutral industrialisation.[46]

There are four ways that this toolkit is different to others in the context of AI and professional services. First, its focus on mid-sized law and accounting firms. Such firms may not have the resources to explore and make decisions about AI readiness, whether in terms of expertise, partner time, investment capital or external partnerships. Second, the toolkit combines several distinct bodies of knowledge, including: management research into business models and business model innovation; studies of professional services firms; operations management; and using scenarios to explore possible futures. Recognising the limitations of design approaches that focus on being 'empathetic' with 'users', it is nevertheless necessary to understand and explore the systems of value creation, and how firms operationalise technologies, to design and develop a viable AI strategy. Third, in developing this toolkit we have drawn on academic research which contextualises, analyses and critiques technology adoption, business models, innovation and design. Using this research base helps us make grounded claims about the utility of the tools and methods offered. Fourth, we developed the toolkit in the context of a multi-partner project involving engagement with a range of firms and stakeholders.

The presentation and description of the methods and tools in this toolkit are informed by our experiences of trialling them in single firm and multi-firm workshops in 2019 and 2020. The result of combining these distinctive contributions is that the toolkit is based on insights and experience relating to the changes and approaches required to adopt AI, how firms create value and future uncertainties faced by professional services firms. In summary, you can think of this toolkit as a recipe that uses a 'design thinking' approach to mix the main ingredients of insights about AI, business models, organisational change, operations and futures into a unique, bespoke dish that your firm can prepare, consume and digest. Using this toolkit, in whole or in part, will support generative, participatory exploration of AI readiness in your firm, drawing on colleagues' expert knowledge and building on rigorous academic research.

34 Liedtka (2020) p. 55.
35 Björklund et al. (2020) p. 101.
36 For an introduction to design thinking see Brown (2009) and Liedtka (2020).
37 thehardcopy.co/design-swarm-ready-get-set-post-it/
38 www.ibm.com/design/approach/design-thinking/
39 www.fjordnet.com/
40 www.ey-seren.com/
41 www.agilealliance.org/agile101/the-agile-manifesto/
42 Knapp et al. (2016).
43 www.mckinsey.com/business-functions/mckinsey-digital/our-insights/how-concept-sprints-can-improve-customer-experience-innovation
44 openpolicy.blog.gov.uk/about/
45 sprintstories.com/the-cidc-design-sprint-233704b3de8d
46 re-industrialise.climate-kic.org/design-sprint-post/about-the-handbook/

2 Exploring AI and your firm through the collaborative design sprint

2. Exploring AI and your firm through the collaborative design sprint

2.1	**How to organise a design sprint**		**41**
2.2	**Remote, in-person or hybrid?**		**43**
2.3	**Who to involve in your design sprint**		**44**
2.4	**Sample agendas**		**46**
	2.4.1	Agenda 1: One-day design sprint	46
	2.4.2	Agenda 2: Multi-day design sprint	46
2.5	**Methods, tools and templates**		**50**
	M0	Define a sprintable challenge	**52**
	M1	Icebreaker	**57**
	M2	Understand your business model	**59**
	M3	Learning from practice	**60**
	M4	Explore future scenarios	**62**
	M5	Bring the future firm to life	**71**
	M6	Explore ai opportunities	**73**
	M7	Start the innovation roadmap	**74**
	M8	Define the innovation beneficiaries	**80**
	M9	Rapid idea generation	**84**
	M10	Make and review models and mock-ups	**87**
	M11	Storyboarding	**90**
	M12	Get 360-degree feedback	**93**
	M13	Complete the innovation roadmap	**94**
	M14	Make presentations and share feedback	**96**
	M15	So what? Now what?	**99**
	M16	Reflective conversation	**101**

The sprint methodology described in this toolkit can be adapted to a range of contexts and in response to different challenges or opportunities. To support this, we offer guidance below on who to involve in the design sprint and how to use the toolkit to achieve a business goal. We also include sample agendas for one-day and for three-week sprint sessions, which obviously fix the time commitment differently and can be adapted to your context, problem definition and priorities.

Image: Glenn Carstens Peters on Unsplash

2.1 How to organise a design sprint

The core of this toolkit is based on the design sprint, a widely used innovation method. The method utilises co-creation to find solutions for complex problems and, as mentioned above, is a time-bounded commitment. Getting value from the insights and expertise embedded in this toolkit requires that you have the following in place:

- A challenge you want to explore that is relevant, timely and agreed with key stakeholders
- A small sprint team willing to try out a new approach
- A broader group of internal (and possibly external) stakeholders to whom that challenge matters, and who are willing to invest time and other resources by participating in the sprint
- An organisation with sufficient absorptive capacity to digest and make sense of the ideas, insights, dialogues and connections that emerge from the sprint
- Resources such as time allocated for people to organise the sprint and budget for paying facilitators or other support professionals, if required
- An agreed timeframe for the sprint process
- Clarity about how outputs and outcomes from the sprint process will feed into other activities in the life of the firm.

2.2

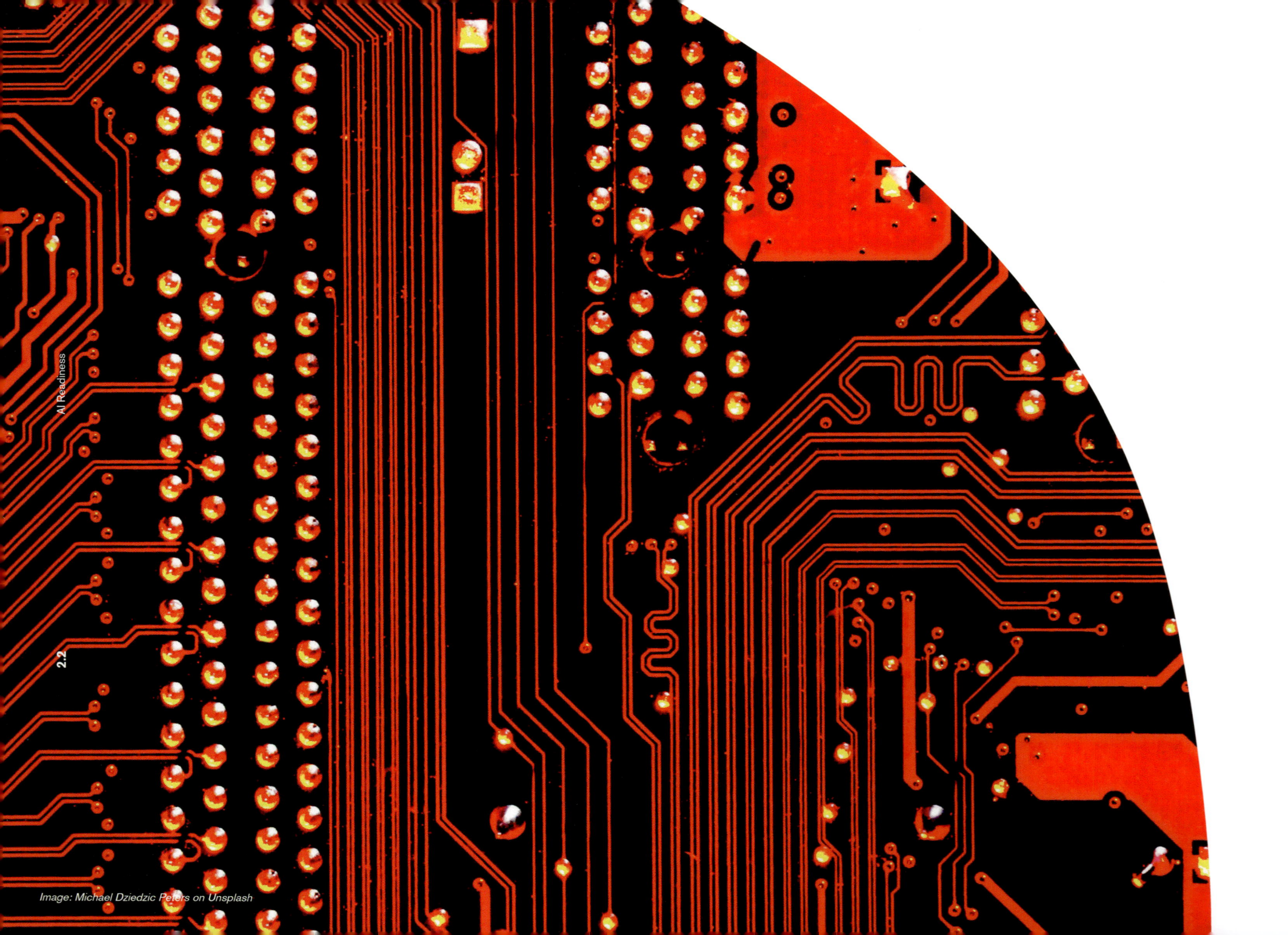

2.2 **Remote, in-person or hybrid?**

The range of contexts in which you might consider running a design sprint now necessarily includes the need to involve some or all participants remotely. It is unlikely that there will be a return to practices and activities that were standard before the COVID-19 pandemic any time soon; and, indeed, that may never happen due to the consequences of rapid digitalisation triggered by the pandemic. Designers and design thinking facilitators have adapted the design sprint to work remotely or through a hybrid of remote and in-person participation. By combining online tools such as Zoom, MS Teams, Miro and Mural, and with some additional planning, it is possible to deliver an effective design sprint regardless of where your teams are physically located. It is now good practice to assume that at least some of your sprint participants will be joining via online tools and, as with all accessibility issues, a little investment upfront can greatly reduce problems later.

If you plan to run the sprint from a central office in which more than two participants will be based, in addition to observing ongoing social distancing and disinfection guidelines, consider getting a bigger room if possible and using high-quality microphones, large screen TVs and wide-angle webcams to ensure the best possible experience for everyone in the sprint, as in any hybrid or online-only business meeting. Consider also using social media tools such as WhatsApp or Slack to facilitate conversation among participants during the sprint. With their agreement, you can capture and save these 'chats', as some of the best ideas emerge from informal conversation. The role of the Documenter outlined below takes on added significance in remote and hybrid sprints, and it is a good idea to ask everyone to contribute by taking as many pictures as possible on their phones and uploading them to a shared folder. The sprint Assistant could also act as a nominated liaison to ensure that remote participants are always kept in the loop during the process.

Finally, don't overlook the additional cognitive load that remote participation imposes. Schedule frequent short breaks and encourage participants to stand up and move around, drink water, and have nutritious snacks available. There are plenty of resources, case studies and how-to tips for remote and hybrid sprints online. See, for example:

The Sprint Book - The Remote Design Sprint Guide
www.thesprintbook.com/remote
Accessed 1st January 2021

UX Collective - How to run great remote workshops
www.uxdesign.cc/how-to-run-great-remote-workshops-da4720777bbe
Accessed 1st January 2021

InVision - How to facilitate a successful remote workshop
www.invisionapp.com/inside-design/facilitating-remote-workshops
Accessed 1st January 2021

Other links and ideas are included within the method descriptions in this toolkit.

2.3 Who to involve in your design sprint

There are several roles you need to fill in order to run a design sprint. You may find that you have people across the organisation with relevant skills, but you may also want to engage external professionals to support the process. While the same individual can play more than one role, the following roles represent a minimum participation requirement to run an effective sprint:

- Sponsor - to define and articulate the challenge the sprint will address, and to allocate resources
- Leader - to mobilise the necessary people and resources, and develop and deliver the activities within an agreed timeframe
- Facilitator - someone skilled in working with plenary and small groups who will adapt the exercises in this toolkit for the context of the firm
- Assistant - to support the leader and facilitator with preparation and delivery
- Documenter - to ensure that the sprint and associated documentation are recorded, captured, labelled and stored through, e.g., note taking, video of plenary discussions, templates filled out by participants and general photography.

Participants should come from across the organisation or organisations involved. When inviting participants, consider these questions:

- Who has a good understanding of the challenge we aim to address?
- Who has insights into emerging market behaviours, including among young people and their use of technology?
- Who is close to current and future clients?
- Who has insights from other industries or sectors?
- Who has expertise or insights into AI and data and how these might be changing in the firm or the profession?
- How will we ensure our commitments to Equality, Diversity and Inclusivity are maintained?
- Who can we invite to be a provocateur or 'irritant', to challenge assumptions?

The exact make-up of participants by role or function will depend on the nature of your challenge. The following indicative lists may be helpful, starting with fee earners at all levels, particularly:

- Director/Managing Director
- Managing Partner
- Senior Partner
- Senior Accountant
- CFO
- Barrister
- Solicitor
- Chartered legal executive and/or fee-earning paralegal
- Practice area/team lead.

And a cross-section of support functions, e.g.:
- CTO and/or IT experts/champions
- Business development
- Innovation management
- Risk management
- Communications
- Policy
- Compliance
- Trainees.

However, it may not be possible to include everyone at every step of the sprint. Your specific needs will naturally inform decisions about who needs to be part of everything and who might be able to contribute via a limited involvement. For example, not everyone may need to read all the background information offered in Section 3 'Understanding the Landscape', but everyone may need to have a good understanding of business models and business model innovation. Similarly, it may be that a core part of the design sprint team is involved in completing all activities, with the managing partner, chief executive or other decision maker less involved, but present at specific stages, such as choosing the focus of the innovation to ensure feasibility and securing 360-degree feedback. Further, the CIO or IT experts and/or software engineers may need to be more involved at certain points. These could include the 2030 Scenario discussions, AI Opportunity Cards activity and Innovation Roadmap exercises. However, if involving specific people at different stages is not possible, the design sprint team should be encouraged to think about opportunities and challenges from the missing people's perspectives: What would a paralegal need to think about or consider in this case? What might the CIO or compliance team need? And so on.

Image: Fauxels on Pexels

2.4 **Sample agendas**

These agendas are for the sprint facilitators' use. They help the delivery team coordinate the range of activities and their sequencing and interactions, so that the sprint process achieves its intended outcomes whilst also remaining open to new or unexpected connections. In addition to these facilitators' agendas, you will need to create an agenda for other sprint participants, which won't require as much detail. Whether you intend to run the sprint in a day or over a longer period, you will need to schedule time ahead of the sprint itself to brief senior stakeholders, recruit and brief participants, prepare detailed agendas and secure the necessary resources (time in people's diaries, administrative and technical support, etc.)

Remote but not forgotten

These agendas were created at a time when gathering everyone in one room was unproblematic - at least, in the sense that it has become problematic since the COVID-19 pandemic. They are included here purely for reference, to give an idea of the timings, flow and outputs of the design sprint process, and help sprint facilitators think about their options. Some notes about remote participation have been added, and facilitators may want to consider what additional planning, infrastructure and resources they might need to ensure that everyone gets an equal opportunity to participate, regardless of location. A little extra technical resource could prevent the loss of a great deal of human resource.

2.4.1 Agenda 1
One-day design sprint

Use this agenda when:
- You can clear diaries to have dedicated space and time for working together
- You have a relatively small group of people who will work through the sprint.

NB: The first method, **M0** Define a sprintable challenge, should be completed and shared with all participants, ideally a week before the actual sprint.

2.4.2 Agenda 2
Multi-day design sprint

Use this agenda when:
- It's hard to get diaries aligned to free up a whole day but plausible to carve out a little time over several days
- You want to draw on a wider group of people.

2.4.1 Agenda 1 One-day design sprint

Indicative timing	Method	Activity	Tools, template and other materials	Who leads
09:00- 09:30		Registration		Assistant
09:30-09:45		Welcome/introduction		Sponsor, Leader
09:45-10:00	M1	Icebreaker		Facilitator
10:00- 10:45	M2	Understand your business model	Business model template	Facilitator
10:45-11:30	M3	Learning from practice	Current Uses of AI	Facilitator leader
11:30-11:45	BREAK			
11:45- 12:15	M5	Bring the firm's future to life	Future Media Artefacts Template	Facilitator
12:15- 12:45	LUNCH			
12:45- 13:15	M6	Explore AI opportunities	AI Opportunity Cards	Facilitator
13:15- 13:45	M7	Start the Innovation Roadmap	Innovation Roadmap	Facilitator
13:45- 14:00	M8	Define the innovation beneficiaries	Persona Cards, Post-It notes, shared editable screen	Facilitator
14:00- 14:15	M9	Rapid idea generation	Paper, pens, equivalent online collaboration tools	Facilitator
14:15-14:45	M11	Storyboarding	Visual Icon Library, Storyboard Template	Facilitator
14:45- 15:00	BREAK			
15:00-15:30	M13	Complete the Innovation Roadmap	Innovation Roadmap	Facilitator, leader, other steakholders
15:30-16:00	M14	Presentations / feedback		Teams
16:15-16:45	M15	So What? Now What?	Flip chart and/or Post-it notes, virtual whiteboards	Facilitator
16:45- 17:00	M16	Reflection/discussion: wrap up		Sponsor, Leader

2.4.2 Agenda 2 Multi-day design sprint

Timeline	Method	Activity	Tools, template and other materials	Who leads	Documenter to capture materials during the sprint
8 weeks before	M0	Define and agree sprintable challenge		Sponsor, Leader	
6 weeks before		Recruitment and briefing of participants		Leader, Facilitator	
3 weeks before		Produce session materials		Leader, Assistant Documenter	
Day 1		Welcome/introduction/set up		Sponsor, Leader	
	M1	Icebreaker		Facilitator leader	
	M2	Understand your business model	Business model template	Facilitator	Photograph each template
		Discussion		Leader	Video the discussion
Day 2	M3	Learning from practice	Current uses of AI		
		Discussion and insight sharing		Facilitator	Video the discussion
Day 3	M4	Explore future scenarios			
		Discuss the 2030 scenarios	Future Scenario Posters	Facilitator, Leader	Video the discussion
	M5	Bring the firm's future to life			
		Show and tell - future artefacts	Future artefacts template	Facilitator	Photograph completed templates
Day 4	M6	Explore AI opportunities	AI opportunity cards	Facilitator	
Day 5	M7	Start the Innovation Roadmap			
		Explore business model innovation from AI	Innovation Roadmap template	Facilitator	Photograph each template
		Design the AI-enabled firm or service		Facilitator	

Timeline	Method	Activity	Tools, template and other materials	Who leads	Documenter to capture materials during the sprint
Day 6	M8	Define the innovation beneficiaries	Persona template and cards	Facilitator	
		Create benefit statements	Post-It notes, editable shared screen		Photograph completed persona templates and benefit statements
Day 7	M9	Rapid idea generation	Paper, pens, equivalent online collaboration platform tools	Facilitator	Photograph rapid idea sheets
	M10	Make and review models and mock-ups	Modelling materials	Facilitator, Leader	
	M11	Storyboarding			
		Make a comic strip	Visual Icon Library and Comic Strip Template	Facilitator	Photograph completed comic strips
Day 8	M12	Get 360-degree feedback		Facilitator, Leader, Sponsor and other stakeholders	Video the feedback and discussion
Day 9-10	M13	Complete the Innovation Roadmap			
		Review the change implications and complete Innovation Roadmap	Innovation Roadmap Tamplates from day 5	Facilitator, Leader	Photograph completed Innovation Roadmaps
Day 11	M14	Presentations, feedback and discussion		Facilitator, Leader	Video the presentations and feedback
Day 12	M15	So What? Now What?	Flip chart and/or Post-it notes, virtual	Facilitator	Video the discussion, photograph
Day 13	M16	Reflective conversation	Flip chart, paper, virtual whiteboard as needed	Facilitator, Leader	Video discussion and capture any notes

2.5 **Methods, tools and templates**

The methods, tools and templates that make up the design sprint are set out here in the order in which they appear in the sample agendas. There is a logic to this order, certainly in the context of the complete design sprint process, and it was successfully tested with professional services firms across the UK in 2019-2020. Thus, the insights gleaned by the facilitators and shared by the participants all contribute to the viability of this design sprint format for AI readiness in professional services. But there is no rule that says you can't change anything. A significant part of the reason why design thinking, and other design-related workshops, have been so successful in recent years is the spirit of curiosity they engender. Not only do workshop structures and individual methods survive being adapted or swapped around, but they can also thrive on such creativity. Feel free to experiment but keep a clear eye on your intended outcomes and maintain a commitment to the shared learning process that makes collaborative design so valuable. The first method is designated **'M0'** simply because it is used ahead of the design sprint itself. To be clear, we use the term 'method' here in the sense of "a systematic way to approach an issue, which in some cases helps deepen understanding of an issue, or helps with ordering or organising it, so a project can move forward".[47] There are also tools and templates to use with some of the methods.

In the process of setting up a sprint and employing these methods, think about the potential number of people involved and whether they are likely to be participating in a shared physical location, remotely via online tools, or in some hybrid of physical and online. Some of the following methods need adaptation for online-only and hybrid situations, particularly group activities. We have made suggestions for adaptations to virtual settings, but, throughout the sprint process, it will be the sprint Leader's decision to determine how best to handle this. Naturally, there's a new buzzword attached to this - OMO (Online Merges with Offline). OMO originated in the retail industry as "a strategy designed to improve customer experience by providing an integrated service that transcends the boundary between the online and offline worlds".[48] Some general OMO advice is offered in Section 2.2 'Remote, in-person or hybrid?' and some specific tips are included within the methods themselves.

47 Kimbell (n.d.).

48 Hoshino (2019).

Image: Brandi Redd Unsplash

M0 Define a sprintable challenge

1. Purpose
To define the problem, issue, opportunity or challenge that will be structured and addressed through the design sprint, allowing participants to explore the potential and implications of AI for professional services firms.

2. Duration
The process of defining the sprint focus is iterative, to allow for refinement and consensus to be achieved. There will likely be a series of meetings, activities and discussions over a period of up to one month, taking place well before the actual sprint.

3. What you need
- People with different perspectives on the organisation (or in relation to the topic, issue or opportunity) and what is going on in and around it, and in the external environment
- Senior buy-in to legitimise engaging with people and using resources such as time.
- A way to capture, review and share ideas, e.g., platforms enabling digital remote collaboration many of which have tools and frameworks you can adopt and refine to suit your own purposes.

4. How to prepare
Read the cases and approaches included in Section 3 of this toolkit to get a grounding in how professional services firms are implementing AI and what changes are required to do this. Read the future scenarios in Section 4 to explore some of the factors that could shape the context in which professional services firms might find themselves operating in the future.

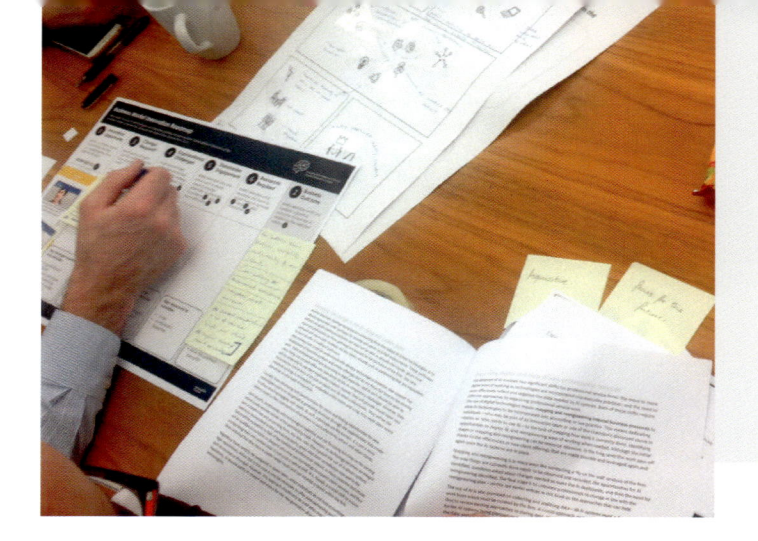

5. How to run this activity

The suggested output of this process is a 'sprintable challenge' statement focusing on the potential and implications of AI for professional services firms, specifically law and accounting firms, using the format below:

> **How can we......
> [use/develop a specific opportunity associated with AI] to result in......
> [changed behaviour or work practice] in order to...... [achieve business goal in professional services firm]?**

To get to this place, the following steps are recommended. For the person or small group leading this activity, what is required is providing the right balance between imposing a structure and being open to what happens. Too much structure can close down the space of exploration, marginalise important perspectives (especially those that go against the grain or challenge shared assumptions), and foreclose possibilities. Too much emergence can result in people experiencing the effort to define the challenge as woolly or wasteful of resources.

Defining the challenge requires:

- Connecting the discussion about AI that will be activated through the design sprint with existing (or emergent) strategic plans, objectives and investments (e.g., strategy development or specific initiatives relating to technology including AI, innovation, partnerships, business development or talent management)
- Inviting in and acknowledging diverse and contrary perspectives
- Agreeing a scope.

Activities that can help you to define your sprintable challenge include:

- Reviewing desk research (collating, reading, annotating, synthesising and discussing key internal and external documents and reports)
- Carrying out and summarising insights from brief interviews with key stakeholders asking them to contribute to creating the challenge by sharing perspectives on problems, opportunities and issues and barriers to change
- Using the 'five whys' method to drill down into a problem statement by asking, 'why is this a problem… and why is that a problem?' (repeating five times)
- Creating an online 'jam board' and inviting participants to (a) input, (b) order/organise and (c) prioritise different understandings of challenges they think AI might help with
- Visualising issues, opportunities and challenges facing the professional services firm (and its clients) through mind-mapping.

When you finalise your challenge statement, you may want to write up the rationale for defining it in this way, drawing on your analysis and discussion of external and internal resources, illustrating it with charts, graphs, screenshot and photographs to add specificity. Examples of challenges used during the development and testing of this toolkit include:

- How might we use our data to decrease employee contact time with clients whilst also enhancing client satisfaction?
- How might we enhance our client services and processes to improve efficiency and enhance client satisfaction?

Business Owner
Wears multiple hats covering all business functions, juggling responsibilities and making

Activity 10: Share and review
Task - Short presentation (10 mins):

6. Output
A written (and possibility illustrated) definition of the challenge.

7. Outcome
A shared understanding of an issue or opportunity that colleagues want to explore further, and that the design sprint methodology is well-placed to address.

8. Background
Defining the challenge is a crucial task, to be done before organising the design sprint. Creating it will probably involve several meetings and discussions to produce a statement that connects the firm with potential opportunities associated with AI in the context of changing professional services. However, even approaching the process of defining the sprint challenge requires thinking about, starting with the word 'problem', which assumes a solution. Other words - such as 'issue', 'opportunity' or 'challenge' - are not necessarily any better as potential alternatives, each carrying their own histories, meanings and implications. For example, in the field known as operations research there have been decades in which researchers have studied ways to do 'problem-structuring',[49] which is essentially what this phase is trying to achieve in order to maximise value from the sprint effort.

A first insight from these research discussions is that problems result from collective dialogue and consensus, rather than appearing ready formed. This is why a series of purposeful and planned discussions can agree the sprint focus as an important preparatory activity. A single person deciding on and building the sprint around what they see as 'the challenge' is less likely to be as impactful as having an agreed approach and could unravel as participants debate the focus rather than moving through the activities to work on it. A second insight is that participants play important roles in using their own knowledge to describe and analyse an issue the sprint can address. That's why it's a good idea to engage a disparate range of views in the definition process. A third is that problem-structuring methods often assume it is better to produce suggestions to improve the situation which are politically feasible and implementable, rather than coming up with optimal solutions that may not get implemented. What this means is that when agreeing the focus for the design sprint, it's better not to restrict thinking to just those challenges which feel solvable or manageable.

Opportunities for innovation can come through the sprint process by going outside existing ways of thinking. Finally, participants learn together from describing the problem situation, and in so doing build up capacity to address uncertainties in the business environment. Whilst defining the challenge is essential preparation for the sprint, the definition process alone can yield positive outcomes and should be taken seriously. Building on these four insights, we use the word 'challenge' in this toolkit to capture the sense that an organisational issue to be discussed, analysed and addressed through AI is in need of a focused and strategic piece of work, which the design sprint offers, as a collaborative design methodology.

However, having said that, not all challenges are amenable to being addressed by the design sprint format. By including the word 'sprintable' in the title of this method we acknowledge the requirement to define and agree a challenge that is meaningful to colleagues and partners in the organisation (and beyond), and which is addressable through the specific characteristics of the tools, methods and templates in this toolkit. A challenge that can be addressed by the design sprint methodology needs to:

- Be neither too broad, nor too narrow. An example of a challenge that is too broad would be one that opens up extensive debate or acknowledges huge uncertainty, such as 'the future of the profession' or 'new regulations on compliance'. An example of one that is too narrow would be one tied to a specific AI platform or provider. A well-specified challenge statement might define an area of the business, or market segment, or client type (and hence be connected to current operations), on which there are likely to be different opinions and options, but in response to which it can be agreed that it is a topic worth working on.

- Connect to an agreed business goal. In order for the design sprint to be meaningful enough for participants to get involved and for resources to be allocated, it should be tied to existing priorities. Whether these are growing an area of the business, reducing costs to deliver for clients, or increasing efficiencies in how people's knowledge is used, a business goal provides the rationale for the design sprint to respond to.

- Align with the firm's timeframes for strategy and planning. It might be that the organisation has recently renewed its strategy or is about to do so. In either case, planning and organising the design sprint to connect with, support, accelerate or complement other work in the organisation will increase efficiencies and buy-in.

49 Smith and Shaw (2019).

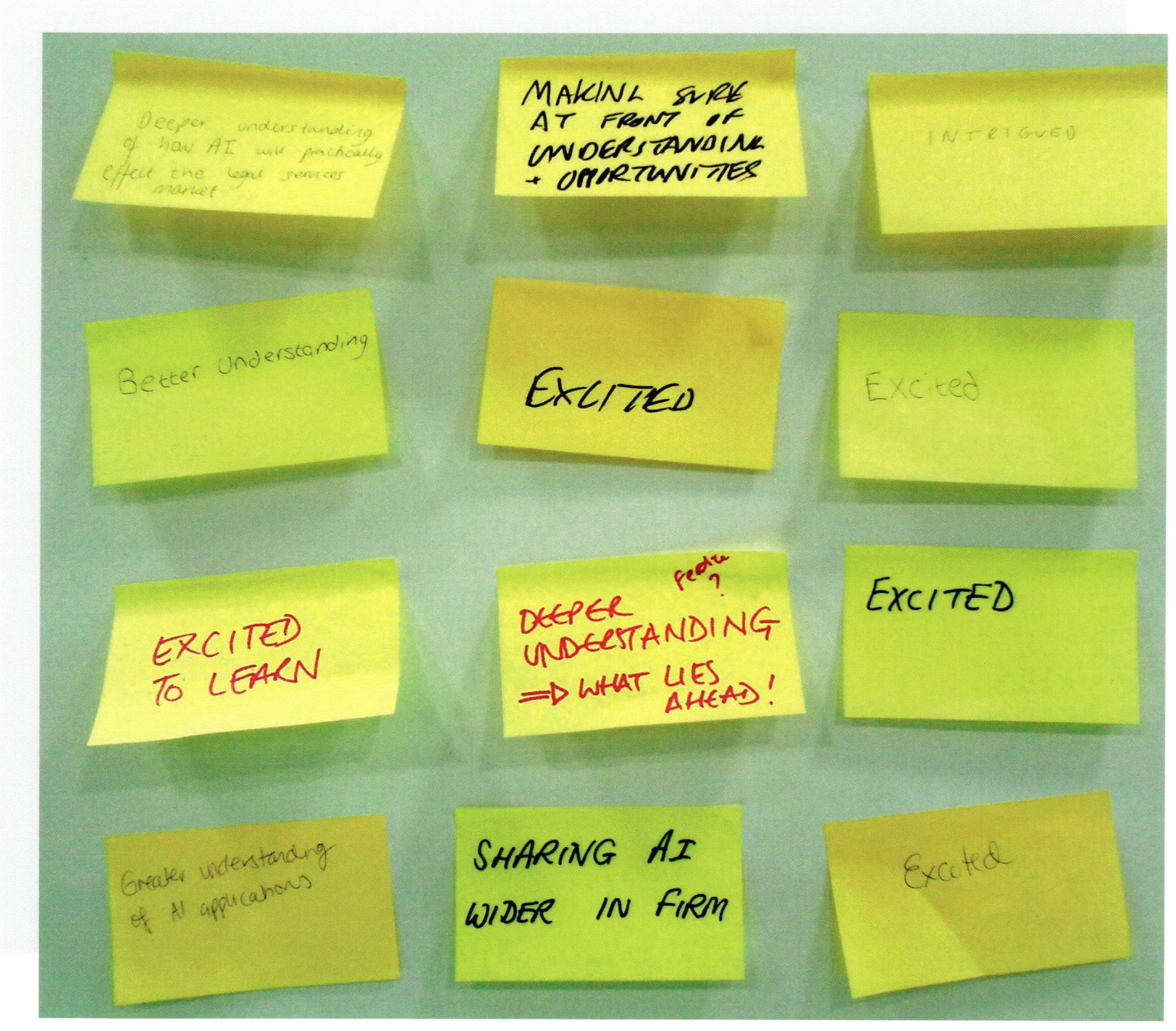

Examples of Icebreaker Post-It notes

M1 Icebreaker

1. Purpose
To stimulate openness in the group and create connections between participants.

2. Duration
5-10 minutes.

3. What you need
Timer and Post-It notes (or shared editable screen).

4. How to prepare
No preparation.

5. How to run this activity
If sharing a room, ask participants to move from where they are sitting and find another person. If working online, consider running this exercise via WhatsApp or other smartphone-based messaging tool. Each participant should introduce themselves to their chosen/designated partner and briefly say what they hope to get out of the design sprint. Give them one minute for each person (2 x one minute).

Then ask each participant to introduce the person they met to the wider group, giving them about one minute each. Optional extra: Following this, give participants two Post-It notes of different colours. You can brief participants to have these at home if they are participating remotely. Ask them to answer briefly the following questions, one question per Post-It note:
- What's your current mood?
- What do you hope to get out of the day?

Collect all Post-Its, read them out, and stick them on the wall in two (colour coded) groups if co-located, or ask participants to type their notes on to colour-coded sections of a shared editable screen. Invite participants to review these during the day by walking past the relevant space occasionally if co-located or visiting the relevant area of your online collaborative platform. In your closing plenary you can also come back to them, and check if the mood has changed as a result of the sprint, and whether people got what they wanted from the day.

6. Output
Notes.

7. Outcome
A team with a shared purpose, warmed to the process ahead and ready to run with it.

8. Background
In the opening session of any design sprint, it is critical to engage people who will have very different reasons for being there and who will feel comfortable engaging in different ways. Even if participants all know each other, it's still worth surfacing what they want to get out of the day and bringing this to the group's attention. As a facilitator, too, you will benefit from hearing directly from people about their expectations early on, allowing you to make adjustments in the plan for the sprint. There are many icebreaker games and activities, and you may decide a different activity would better suit your particular group or groups.[50]

[50] See, for instance, Gray et al. (2010).

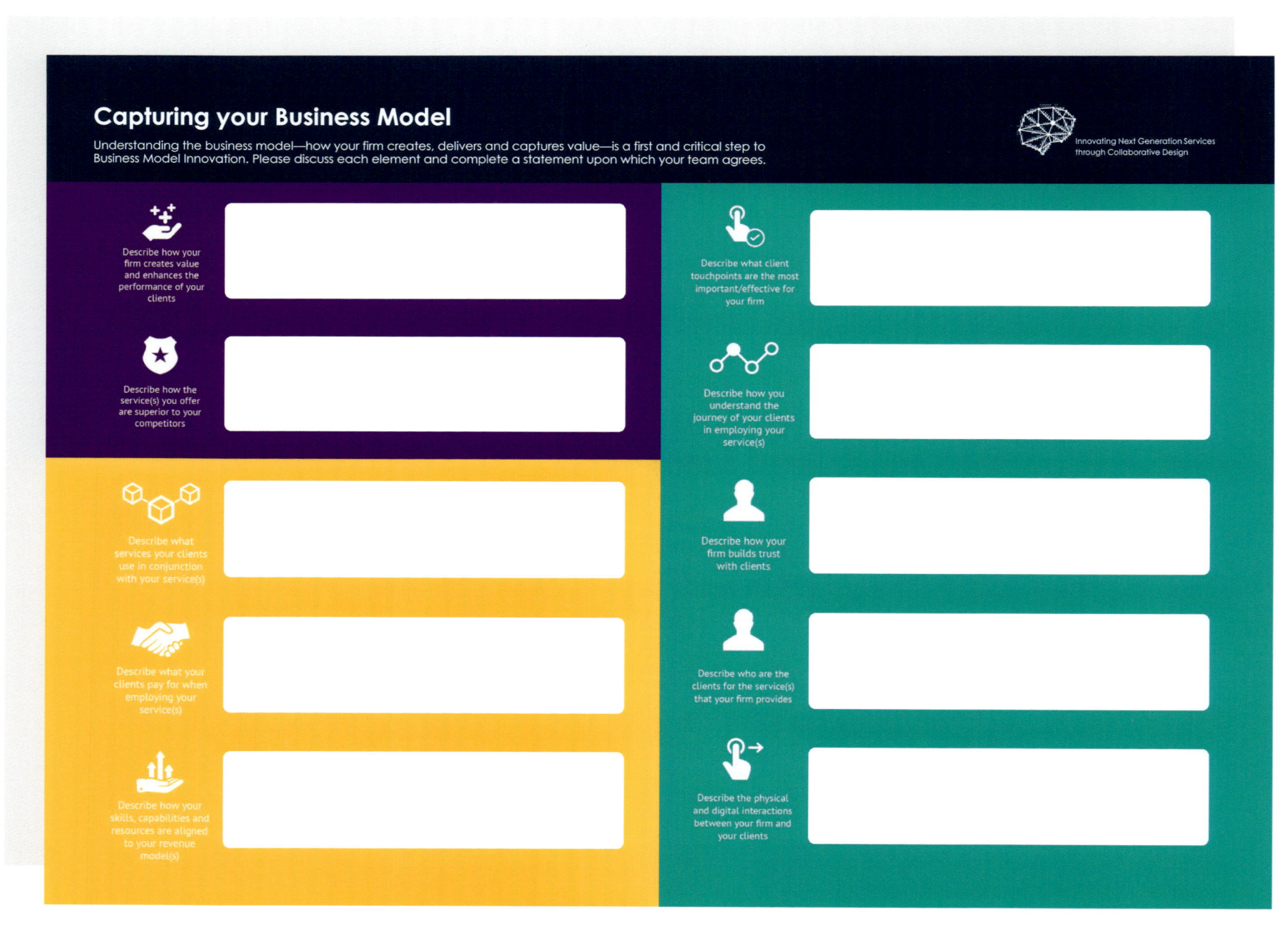

Capturing your Business Model

Understanding the business model—how your firm creates, delivers and captures value—is a first and critical step to Business Model Innovation. Please discuss each element and complete a statement upon which your team agrees.

Innovating Next Generation Services through Collaborative Design

- Describe how your firm creates value and enhances the performance of your clients
- Describe how the service(s) you offer are superior to your competitors
- Describe what services your clients use in conjunction with your service(s)
- Describe what your clients pay for when employing your service(s)
- Describe how your skills, capabilities and resources are aligned to your revenue model(s)
- Describe what client touchpoints are the most important/effective for your firm
- Describe how you understand the journey of your clients in employing your service(s)
- Describe how your firm builds trust with clients
- Describe who are the clients for the service(s) that your firm provides
- Describe the physical and digital interactions between your firm and your clients

Business Model template

M2 Understand your business model

1. Purpose
To understand how your firm creates value.

2. Duration
60 minutes.

3. What you need
M2 Business Model Template.

4. How to prepare
Consider circulating some reading matter or media content sharing discussions of business models, business model innovation and the specifics of these in your sector.

5. How to run this activity
Using the Business Model Template, discuss each element and complete a statement upon which your team agrees. If you have multiple teams participating in the design sprint, ask each team to complete a template. This can provide valuable additional insight and test the shared understanding of the business model. Once you complete these, it will be useful to discuss whether everyone in your firms and/or those involved in the design sprint team have a shared understanding of your firm's business model. In our experience of delivering design sprints, we have observed that individuals operating at different levels in the firm often have different understandings of the business model. Moreover, it is useful to identify early on those areas where your firm is particularly strong or innovative and where AI readiness has the most potential. To aid the discussion, consider the following questions:

- Do you think your firm is particularly innovative or strong in one or more of these areas?
- Where is the most potential for AI to change these areas of the business model?
- Which of the three business model dimensions - experience, configuration, and offering - do you find it easier to think or talk about?
- What was easily agreed? What was contentious?
- Was there consideration of how the dimensions related to each other?
- What surprised you?

6. Output
Completed Business Model Template(s).

7. Outcome
- A shared understanding of how the firm creates value
- Insights in different ways the firm creates value.

8. Background
This is the first in a series of activities designed to support your firm on its AI readiness journey. The purpose of this activity is to help you develop a shared understanding of the core elements of your firm's business model. Understanding the business model - how your firm creates, delivers and captures value - is a first and critical step to Business Model Innovation.

M3 Learning from practice

1. Purpose
To understand how law and accounting firms are adopting and deploying AI.

2. Duration
45 to 60 minutes.

3. What you need
Toolkit sections 3.4 'Current uses of AI in accounting and law firms in England' and 3.5 'Approaches to the deployment of AI in accounting and law firms in England'.

4. How to prepare
Ask participants to read the relevant section before the session.

5. How to run this activity
Invite participants for their initial responses and discuss. Use the following questions to stimulate conversation and help make the research useful for your firm and sector:
- Which cases and approaches to adoption seem most relevant to your firm/sector? Why?
- What would you hope to achieve by using AI if your firm adopted a similar approach to its deployment?
- What do you imagine AI would do? What specific tasks or forms of analysis would it be used for?
- What do you think AI would offer your clients/sector that is better or different to what is currently available?
- What is changing in the sector as a result of AI and what might change?

6. Output
Notes from the discussion and responses to the questions.

7. Outcome
A shared understanding of some of the ways law and accounting firms are adopting and implementing AI and what this might mean for your firm/sector.

8. Background
As part of our research, we carried out interviews with law and accounting firms adopting or implementing AI. The key insights are summarised in section 3.4 'Current uses of AI in accounting and law firms in England'. This activity aims to support participants to articulate these insights to make them useful for your firm. Although the cases may cover sectors or forms of practice that your firm does not offer, they show how different firms have adopted AI and changed as a result, which offers some learning for firms in other sectors.

Image: Christina Morillo on Pexels

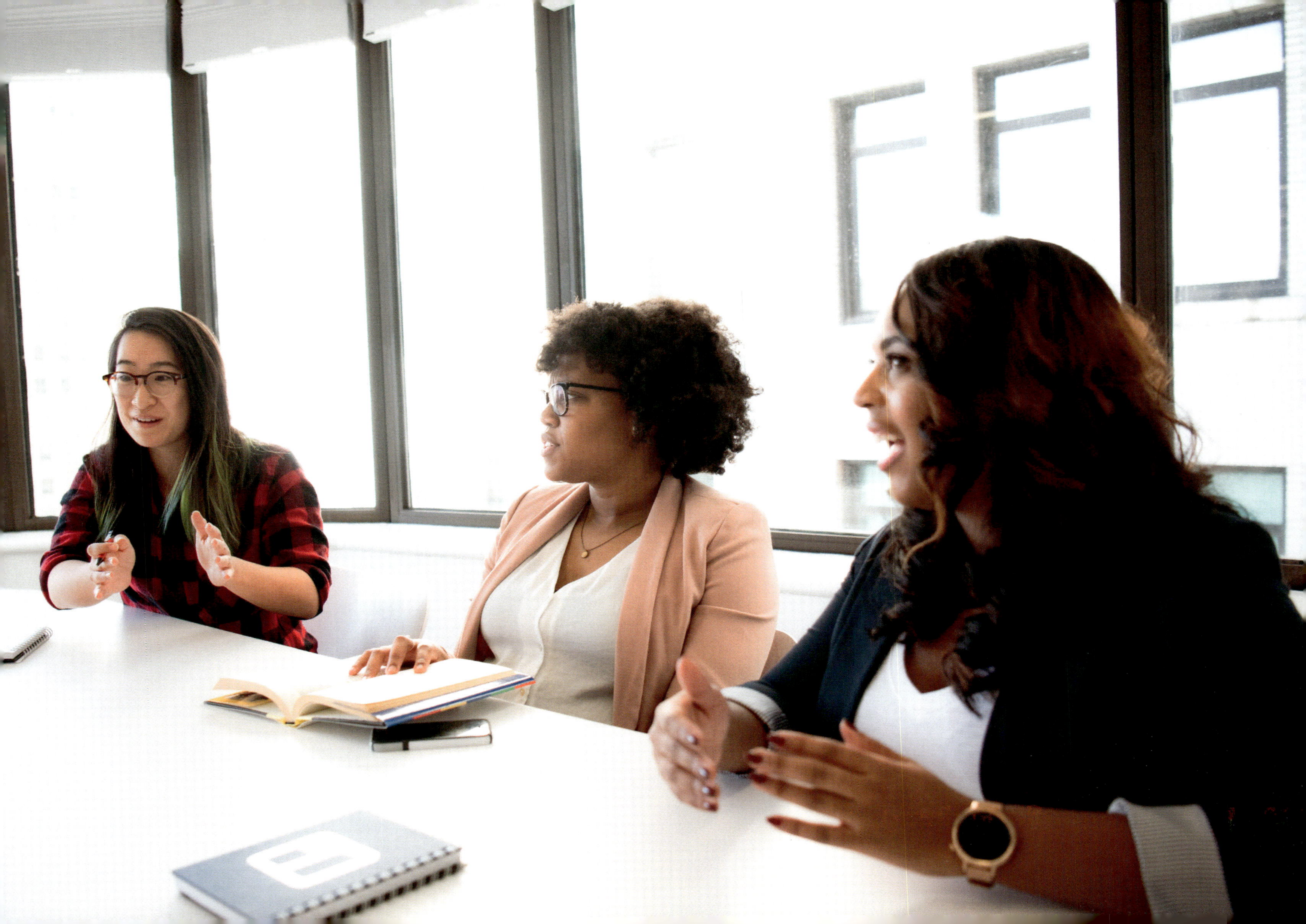

M4 Explore future scenarios

1. Purpose
To explore the strategic implications of three future scenarios.

2. Duration
60 or 120 minutes, depending on options chosen.

3. What you need
- The three 2030 scenarios from section 4.3
- M4 scenario posters
- Session agenda adapted to achieve your aim.

4. How to prepare
- Depending on your colleagues' level of familiarity with AI and its broader potential you may want to circulate a reading or watching list relevant to your market or sector and/or broader issues relating to AI such as data, ethics and privacy to launch a discussion. The scenarios are summarised as posters if you are pressed for time. If you have more time, section 4.3 offers written versions of the scenarios.
- Decide on what you want to use the scenarios for. This will mean that your session design will be different depending on your aims. We give three options below. The first two allow you to explore a conundrum (in two different formats); the third allows you to test an existing strategy by seeing how its key components hold up in each scenario.
- Get clear up front how any work you carry out will intersect with other developments in the firm e.g., strategy reviews or innovation planning.
- When deciding who to invite to participate, ensure you have a mix of perspectives and expertise in the room, making space for diversity in all senses.
- Assign people to sub-groups with a mix of perspectives in each.

5. How to run this activity
There are three options, each organised to achieve a different purpose.

Option 1. Exploring the implications of potential futures (short form)

Purpose
Exploring a complex issue: Participants explore one scenario in depth, the team covers all three.

Duration
One hour.

Agenda
- Intro: Set the scene, introduce the conundrum, explain the workshop method (5 mins)
- Break into three sub-groups for structured discussion of one scenario each (ensuring all three are covered across the sub-groups) (30 mins).
- Task 1: Individual: Participants read the scenario poster (2 mins).
- Task 2: Discuss in break out sub-group: What do you see going on in this world? (5 mins).

Q1. What is there in what your organisation is currently doing (its culture, capabilities, types of clients or work, and the way it is organised) which would mean it would be successful in this world?

Q2. What is there in what your organisation is currently doing (its capabilities, culture, clients, work or ways of organising) which would mean it would NOT be successful in this world?

Q3. If this scenario was going to unfold, does your organisation have the AI capabilities to be successful in this world (for example, access to data, data analytics, machine learning)?

Plenary: Report back from each sub-group (20 mins)
- Summarise key insights from discussing the scenarios
- What will you tell the managing partner (or other leaders)?

Option 2. Exploring implications of potential futures (longer form)

Purpose
Exploring a complex issue: Participants explore all three scenarios, enabling fuller comparisons across them.

Duration
Two hours.

Agenda
- Intro: Set the scene, introduce the conundrum, explain workshop method (15 mins)
- Break into groups all with (the same) scenario (22 mins).
- Task 1: Individual: Participants read the scenario poster (2 mins).
- Task 2: Discuss in break-out group: What do you see going on in this world? (5 mins).
- Task 3: Discuss in break-out group (20 mins).

Q1. What is there in what your organisation is currently doing (and its culture, capabilities, types of clients or work, and the way it is organised) which would mean it would be successful in this world?

Q2. What is there in what your organisation is currently doing (its capabilities, culture, clients, work or ways of organising) which would mean it would NOT be successful in this world?

Plenary: Each sub-group reports back. Compare across the sub-groups (10 min)
- Repeat with scenario 2 (15 min + 10 mins*)
- Repeat with scenario 3 (15 min + 10 mins*)

Plenary (15 mins): Overall learnings and conclusions
- What will you tell the managing partner (or other leaders)?

*The first round needs more time as participants need to familiarise themselves with the method of discussing scenarios.

Image: Michael Dziedzic on Unsplash

These scenarios include eight key aspects, each of which is an important uncertainty that has the potential to significantly change the operating environment.

Option 3. Wind-tunneling an existing strategy

Purpose
Testing how a strategy or plan would perform in potential futures. Participants test components of an existing strategy in all three scenarios.

Duration
Two hours.

Preparation
If you have an AI, tech or innovation strategy, break it up into about five components, described in about one sentence each, and put these in a table. For example, 'We will collaborate with third parties on AI product development rather than developing technology in-house'.

Agenda
- Intro: Set the scene, introduce the strategy and components, explain workshop method (10 mins)
- Sub-groups: First round (30 mins).
- Task 1: Individual: Participants read scenario 1 poster (2 mins).
- Task 2: Discuss in break out group. What do you see going on in this world? (8 mins).
- Task 3: Assess in break-out group. Discuss and assess each of the AI strategy components in this scenario - how will each perform? (approx. 3 mins per component) (20 mins).

Plenary: Each group reports back. Compare across the groups (10 min)

- Repeat with scenario 2 (2 min + 5 min + 15 mins*)
- Repeat with scenario 3 (2 min + 5 min + 15 mins*)

Plenary: Overall learnings and conclusions (15 mins)
- What will you tell the managing partner (or other leaders)?

6. Output
Notes from session with key insights from discussing the strategic implications of each scenario.

7. Outcome
- A shared understanding of a range of uncertainties related to AI in the contextual environment facing your organisation, sector, clients and society as a whole
- More incisive questions to ask about the basis on which decisions are made
- (For option 3) A sense of how current strategies will perform in different plausible scenarios.

8. Background
This toolkit includes three scenarios of 2030 designed to be plausible stories of potential developments in the contextual environment for your firm. These scenarios include eight key aspects, each of which is an important uncertainty that has the potential to significantly change the operating environment. These aspects are:
- Future professionals and their work
- Professional services industry structure
- Societal acceptance of AI
- Technology diffusion
- Data access and management
- Regulation and oversight
- The standing of the professions
- Divergence and convergence between law and accounting
- Global trading and economic environment
- UK economy, politics and international standing.

A scenario describes the future in a systemic way and gives indications about how we might end up there. Scenarios are plausible stories about the future. They are not predictions, nor are they based on the idea of having options to select between, some of which are more preferable than others. Instead, creating and using scenarios enables people in an organisation to explore and discuss potential future worlds your business may find itself in. Through exploring and discussing them, you have an opportunity to think about how these different uncertainties may play out and what this might mean for your firm, market, sector, profession and society as a whole. Scenarios are used to aid creating strategic options, identifying risks, testing strategies and plans ('wind-tunneling'), exploring complex issues and having dialogues with multiple stakeholders. Among the benefits of using and discussing scenarios, participants will have:
- Reflected on the resilience and vulnerability of different options or specific strategic decisions they are considering
- Evaluated the viability of an existing strategy and identified any need for modifications and/or contingency plans
- Gained new insights that can inform a strategy that is robust enough to deal with the wide variations in business conditions across all the scenarios.

2030 Scenarios

Scenario 1 poster: Platform Domination

Platform Domination 2030 Scenario

A WORLD WHERE...
A few 'platform' businesses control access to data infrastructures, setting the rules for everyone else including those needing access to data to train algorithms or automate services

SOCIETAL ACCEPTANCE OF AI
Acceptance of targeted, personalised, media-rich digital experiences underpinned by AI. Democrats and activists worried by surveillance and political messaging

FUTURE PROFESSIONALS AND THEIR WORK
New career opportunities have emerged but there are fewer jobs outside the dominant players

CON/DIVERGENCE BETWEEN LAW AND ACCOUNTING
Differences between law and accounting matter less. The Big Four extend their footprint in law, building on expertise in analysing large data and standardised procedures

DATA ACCESS AND MANAGEMENT
Big platform businesses control and charge for access to centralised data lakes. Small firms risk fraud and fines from using bootleg data

TECHNOLOGY DIFFUSION
Competing standards set by the dominant platforms. Little innovation. **Devices and software are rarely truly global.**

UK ECONOMY, POLITICS, STANDING AND TRADING ENVIRONMENT
A more assertive EU: restrictions on trade in products and services with UK. UK imposes **restrictions on inward/outbound trade**, travel and active border management, except with key partners

PROFESSIONAL SERVICES INDUSTRY STRUCTURE
There are fewer, larger firms, resulting from consolidation. **Small and mid-size firms survive in niches**

REGULATION AND OVERSIGHT
The **big platforms control and charge for access to data for national security and risk management** and have significant lobbying power

STANDING OF THE PROFESSIONS
AI-enabled professional services using **large datasets result in fewer errors and greater consistency**

GLOBAL TRADING AND ECONOMIC ENVIRONMENT
Low growth, with supply chains organised within distinct geo-political trade blocs. A federal EU with several markets with strong protections. Limited international collaboration around regulation and data-sharing – resulting in **the 'splinternet'**

About this world: In 2030, a small number of very large firms - with 'platform' business models - have access to private 'data lakes' used to deliver and customise services across borders and jurisdictions. AI is now invisible and routine, built into many products and services, including the dark web, underpinned by strong regulation. Consumers trust platform firms, but democrats and activists are worried by surveillance and political messaging.

Professional services: AI-enabled professional services firms pay for access to the data lakes, resulting in fewer errors and greater consistency and reliability. This increases the standing of top tier professionals. Small and mid-size professional services firms survive in niches, sometimes creating risks for themselves and clients by using bootleg data resulting in fraud and fines. Profits are thin and innovation is limited.

Scenario 2 poster: Bumpy Superhighway

Bumpy Superhighway 2030 Scenario

A WORLD WHERE...

People are surrounded and targeted by ever-updating, personalised, surveillance-based digital services underpinned by invisible and minimally regulated automated data-sharing and analysis - with uneven outcomes for business and for society

SOCIETAL ACCEPTANCE OF AI
Wide acceptance of automated services AI is embedded in the everyday for consumers, but on a patchy basis

FUTURE PROFESSIONALS AND THEIR WORK
New entrants offer new ways of working attract qualified professionals and others with related skills

CON/DIVERGENCE BETWEEN LAW AND ACCOUNTING
With a shared focus on **solving client problems, and access to combined business datasets and AI tool**s, differences between professions matter less.

DATA ACCESS AND MANAGEMENT
A **new breed of data warehouse** providers manage and store data and provide services

TECHNOLOGY DIFFUSION
Much innovation but **quality varies** as does consumer safety. **Cybersecurity** is a new big issue and opportunity

UK ECONOMY, POLITICS, STANDING AND TRADING ENVIRONMENT
UK offers a **low regulation, pro-investment environment.** International firms, including tech giants and Chinese investors, are free to operate in the UK

PROFESSIONAL SERVICES INDUSTRY STRUCTURE
Consolidation between law, accounting and other professional services in response to new entrants into professional services including tech players

REGULATION AND OVERSIGHT
Multiple and inconsistent frameworks and guidelines

STANDING OF THE PROFESSIONS
AI-augmented advisory and audit services are tied to collaborative professional expertise, rather than individual professions

GLOBAL TRADING AND ECONOMIC ENVIRONMENT
Low or medium growth, but highly uneven. **Tech giants in partnership with local players push digitalisation and datafication into many sectors**

About this world: In a push for economic growth after the Covid recession, the UK government allowed tech giants in partnership with local players to push digitalisation and datafication into many sectors. As a result, in 2030 AI is embedded in the everyday for consumers and for business, but on a patchy basis. The speed at which this happened led to regulatory gaps and missed opportunities to make AI algorithms and data access safe, fair and explainable. Cybersecurity is a new big public policy issue, a business concern with insider and external threats, and dedicated professional specialism. The information superhighway appears to have been realised, but with bumps, pot-holes and limited oversight.

Professional services: Following the opening up of professional services sectors in the early part of the decade, new entrants launched AI-based, non-protected services, benefitting from new business models, deep pockets, strong brands and positive attitudes towards long-term investment. All incumbent professional services firms struggled, leading to consolidation. In 2030, clients benefit from reduced prices and increased quality for professional services. But quality varies, as does consumer safety.

Scenario 3 poster: Value Kaleidoscope

Value Kaleidoscope 2030 Scenario

A WORLD WHERE...

AI is integral to connecting, monitoring, evaluating and auditing organisations and individuals allowing them to achieve business goals aligned with stakeholder value, which is increasingly tied to positive environmental, health and social impacts.

SOCIETAL ACCEPTANCE OF AI
Increased **surveillance** is acceptable for shared social, **health** and **environmental** goals

FUTURE PROFESSIONALS AND THEIR WORK
Millennials exercise their values in clients and professional services. Emphasis on individual **life long learning**, not building up firms

CON/DIVERGENCE BETWEEN LAW AND ACCOUNTING
Regional mid-sized firms **combine local knowledge and networks**, with AI-enabled analysis

DATA ACCESS AND MANAGEMENT
A shift from data privacy to **data sharing** for health and social goals

TECHNOLOGY DIFFUSION
Certified code is monitored and assessed by government.

UK ECONOMY, POLITICS, STANDING AND TRADING ENVIRONMENT
Emerging multi-nation alignment and cross-border regulation on **sustainable growth**. Strong UK policy emphasis and investment on levelling up

PROFESSIONAL SERVICES INDUSTRY STRUCTURE
Clients use **AI-enabled search to find suppliers. Temporary project teams** with varied expertise and local knowledge form to serve clients

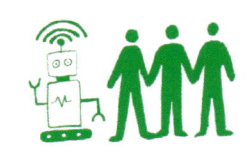

REGULATION AND OVERSIGHT
AI platforms, data access, 'black boxes' and markets are **highly regulated** at international and national levels

STANDING OF THE PROFESSIONS
Specialisation and in-depth expertise are valued. Professional advice is more affordable

GLOBAL TRADING AND ECONOMIC ENVIRONMENT
Low growth, with reduced supply chains involving China. Confident EU. **New levels of co-ordination and regulation among global actors and regional actors**. 'Value' reframed, tied to addressing pandemics, carbon, water and food

About this world: 'Value' has been reframed: it is now tied to addressing pandemics, carbon emissions, and water and food availability, alongside economic growth, achieved within a new political alignment on working collaboratively and sharing data in common formats. Organisations using AI operate within common rules and standards with strong governance. Regulated AI is now built into products and services, underpinned by global monitoring, compliance and reporting, accessible to small and medium-sized businesses and public services.

Professional services: In 2030 clients routinely identify and engage with potential suppliers and advisors using platforms underpinned by regulated AI to assemble teams to meet their needs for professional services. Full service firms have lost their advantage, and there are more opportunities for small and mid-size firms. There is reduced profitability for all professional services firms. The value-add of professionals is at the forefront of people's minds, in an environment in which clients can easily adjust their requirements and preferences, reconfiguring the kaleidoscope of providers and professionals.

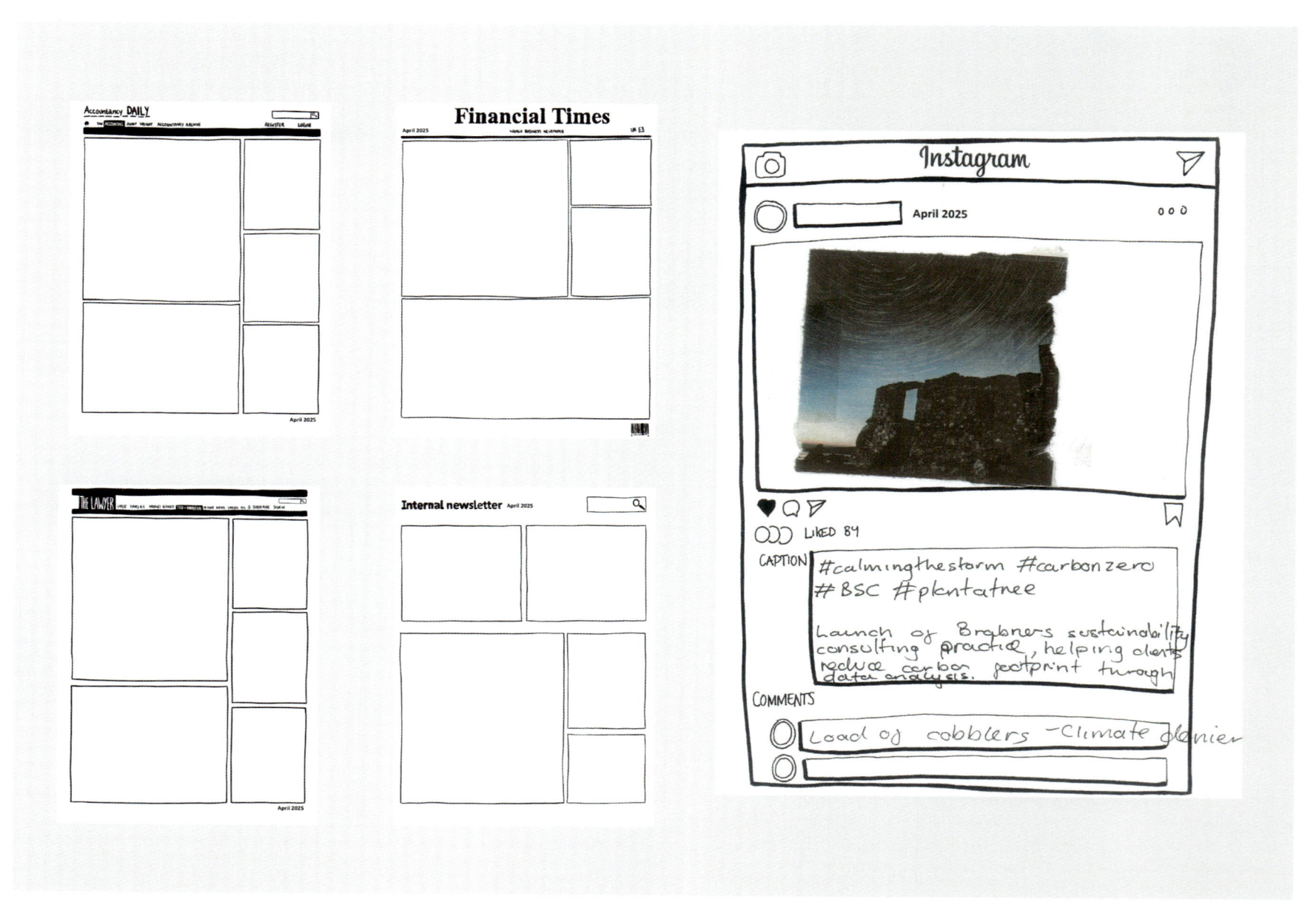

Media & Social Media templates

Instagram caption:
#calmingthestorm #carbonzero #BSC #plantatree

Launch of Brabners sustainability consulting practice, helping clients reduce carbon footprint through data analysis.

Comments:
Load of cobblers — Climate denier

M5 Bring the future firm to life

1. Purpose
To bring to life aspects of the future firm to generate discussion and new insights.

2. Duration
30 minutes.

3. What you need
- M5 Future Media Artefacts Template
- Some examples of extant media/social media reports on AI, business and professional services.

4. How to prepare
Read and discuss the three 2030 scenarios included in the toolkit in Section 4.3, or the poster versions, which specifically suggest plausible stories of the worlds that professional services firms might be operating within, with a focus on AI and its possibilities and implications. We suggest you use M4 'Explore future scenarios' to carry out a structured discussion of these implications. But you can also get value from jumping straight from reading the scenarios to this method, to bring some of these uncertainties to life to enable discussion.

Carry out desk research to find other examples of futures thinking by professional bodies, think tanks, large consultancies, government and academia. The future is, by definition, unknowable, but creating objects from the future can help bring it to life.

5. How to run this activity
Tell a future story written in 2025 about your firm (or a client you have helped, or a competitor) using AI, with positive or negative outcomes. To tell your story, pick one media template and audience to tell that story to. One of them is a mainstream newspaper, one is for a media publication aimed at professionals, one is a social media channel, and one is a template for an internal firm email or newsletter. Share, compare and discuss the future artefacts you have made and the stories they tell. Reflect on:
- What opportunities result from deploying AI?
- What consequences do you see associated with investments in deploying AI?
- What are the benefits and risks of waiting it out, to see how other firms in your sector use of AI?
- What are the benefits and risks of being an early adopter in your sector, market or profession regarding use of AI?

Options for running this activity include:
- Working individually or in pairs to create the stories
- Creating both negative and positive stories about AI in your firm, profession or sector
- Picking a different year - nearer or further ahead
- Consider re-telling the story for a different audience. For example, if you have focussed on a professional audience, now create another version for a mainstream media publication. How might the same story surface quite different implications for another group of people?

6. Output
Mock-ups of media/social media reports from the future.

7. Outcome
New insights into how the firm (or its clients, partners, regulators and society as a whole) might operate in the future.

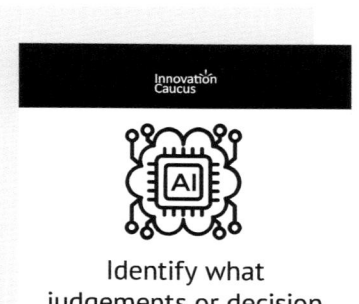

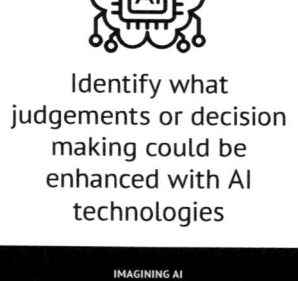

IMAGINING AI cards:

- Identify what judgements or decision making could be enhanced with AI technologies
- Identify new services your firm would develop based on AI technologies
- Identify what processes in your firm could be optimised with AI technologies service(s)
- Describe what tasks or workflows in your firm could be automated with AI technologies
- Describe new clients and markets that could be identified and accessed using AI technologies
- Identify what tasks could be enhanced or enabled with the use of AI technologies
- Describe in what areas you think AI technologies could augment professional expertise
- Describe which of your services could be augmented by AI technologies to provide greater accuracy

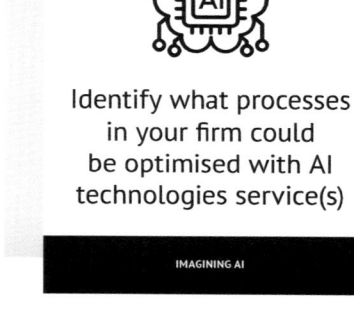

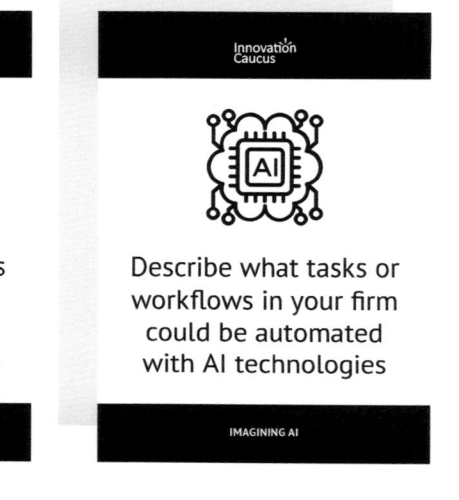

Business Model Innovation cards

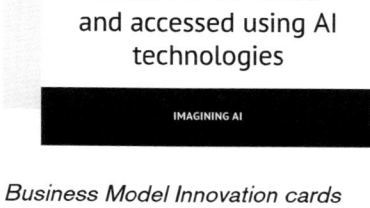

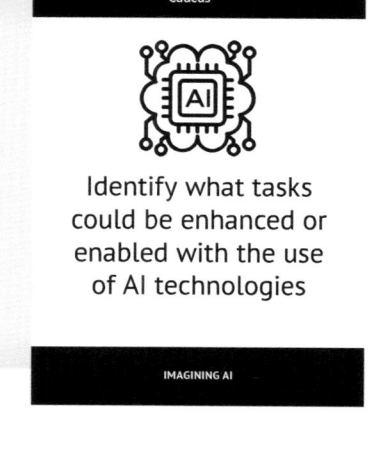

M6 Explore AI opportunities

1. Purpose
To identify opportunities for using AI to change your business model.

2. Duration
30 minutes.

3. What you need
M6 AI Opportunity Cards (Nine in total). These can be shared in a single PDF or as individual image files, both for in-person and remote working.

4. How to prepare
Depending on your colleagues' level of familiarity with AI and its broader potential, you may want to circulate a reading or watching list relevant to your market or sector and/or broader issues relating to AI such as data, ethics and privacy.

5. How to run this activity
Review and discuss the cards. Pick the one(s) that you think are most relevant to your firm. This activity can be completed in groups and each group can then feed their thoughts and insights to the wider team. If you are using this toolkit to explore opportunities for AI adoption or are unsure about AI and it may fit within your firm, these cards can form the basis for exploring opportunities and identifying challenges and solutions.

6. Output
Selected card(s).

7. Outcome
A shared vision for moving forward to explore the potential for AI for your firm.

8. Background
With an understanding of your firm's current business model, you can now think about what AI can do for your business. To help you consider how AI may challenge different dimensions of your existing business model, this toolkit includes a series of AI cards which address different dimensions of the business model, and prompt you to think about aspects such as how AI may augment current work, automate tasks, or disrupt current processes.

M7 Start the Innovation Roadmap

1. Purpose
To develop your firm's Innovation Roadmap.

2. Duration
45 minutes.

3. What you need
- M7 Business Model Innovation Cards
- Printed out or digital copy of the M7 Innovation Roadmap.

4. How to prepare
Read section 1.3.2 'Business models and business model innovation'.

5. How to run this activity
This activity requires you to familiarise yourself with the Business Model Innovation Cards included in the toolkit. To complete this activity, follow these steps:
- Discuss the business model innovation cards in your teams
- Identify the one(s) that seem(s) most important to your firm and to the current business challenge you intend to address.

You can select and focus on one card or multiple cards, depending on the business goals that you want to address and your intended firm outcomes in relation to AI. Once you select your card, focus on this card using the Business Model Innovation Roadmap template below. At this stage, you are only required to complete the last box (Box 2) and define the desired future outcome for the firm resulting from this opportunity. You will come back to the Innovation Roadmap in the following method **M8** 'Define the innovation beneficiaries' to add the intended beneficiary or beneficiaries to the Roadmap; and again, in **M13** 'Complete the Innovation Roadmap' to fill in the remaining sections.

6. Output
Partially completed Innovation Roadmap.

7. Outcome
A shared understanding of the opportunity resulting from AI, the beneficiary or beneficiaries and outcome(s).

8. Background
This activity will support you to develop an innovation roadmap that will guide the development of your AI solution(s). The roadmap template is designed to help you identify your desired AI solution(s) and consider a range of challenges and risks that you may need to address and mitigate in implementing these within your firm.

Innovation Caucus

How can your firm grow their client base for its service(s)

CONFIGURATION | REVENUE MODEL

Innovation Caucus

How can interactions with your clients be made easier?

EXPERIENCE | PHYSICAL & DIGITAL INTERACTION

Innovation Caucus

What new service(s) can your firm offer clients?

OFFERING | VALUE & PERFORMANCE

Start with these 3 Business Model Innovation cards

The full deck of Business Model Innovation cards

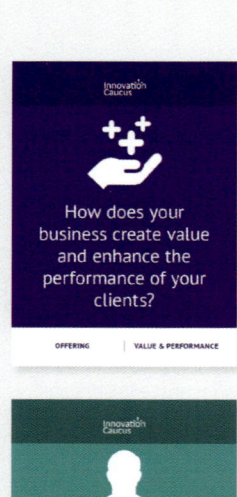

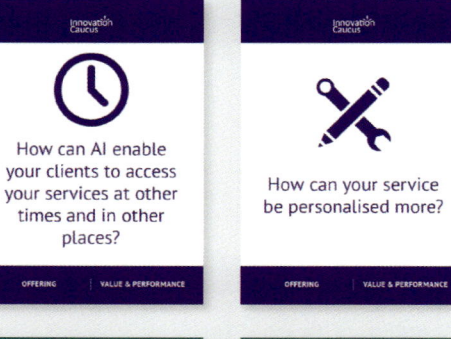

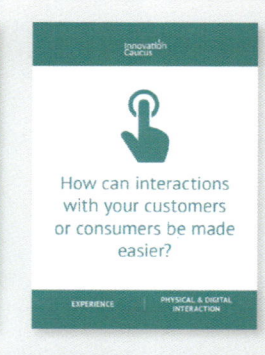

How does your business create value and enhance the performance of your clients? *OFFERING | VALUE & PERFORMANCE*	How is the service you offer superior to your competitors? *OFFERING | VALUE & PERFORMANCE*	How can AI improve the ease of use of the services you provide to clients? *OFFERING | VALUE & PERFORMANCE*	How can AI improve ease of use of the services you offer? *OFFERING | VALUE & PERFORMANCE*	How can AI enable your clients to access your services at other times and in other places? *OFFERING | VALUE & PERFORMANCE*	How can your service be personalised more? *OFFERING | VALUE & PERFORMANCE*
Who are the customers (i.e purchasers) and who are the consumers (i.e. users) of your product/process/service? *EXPERIENCE | PHYSICAL & DIGITAL INTERACTION*	How do your customers experience your services? *EXPERIENCE | PHYSICAL & DIGITAL INTERACTION*	How do your clients interact with you physically and digitally? *EXPERIENCE | PHYSICAL & DIGITAL INTERACTION*	How do you understand your customer journey to purchase and to use? *EXPERIENCE | PHYSICAL & DIGITAL INTERACTION*	How does your business build trust with customers and consumers? *EXPERIENCE | PHYSICAL & DIGITAL INTERACTION*	How does your branding reflect what your business does? *EXPERIENCE | BRAND*
How does your brand convey a promise that is consistently delivered? *EXPERIENCE | BRAND*	What customer touchpoints are the most important/effective for your business now (and in the future)? *EXPERIENCE | CHANNEL*	How can interactions with your customers or consumers be made easier? *EXPERIENCE | PHYSICAL & DIGITAL INTERACTION*	Who is your next new customer? *EXPERIENCE | PHYSICAL & DIGITAL INTERACTION*	How can your business use its brand to reduce customer perception of risk? *EXPERIENCE | BRAND*	How can your business leverage products/processes/services positively associated with your brand? *EXPERIENCE | BRAND*
How can your business benefit from brand extension? *EXPERIENCE | BRAND*	How can your products/processes/services be consumed at different times and in different locations? *EXPERIENCE | CHANNEL*	How can your business connect with end users (consumers) more directly? *EXPERIENCE | CHANNEL*	How can your business enable your customers to interact with one another? *EXPERIENCE | CHANNEL*	How and where do you carry out transactions with your customers? *CONFIGURATION | TRANSACTIONS*	What transactions does your business have with customers? *CONFIGURATION | TRANSACTIONS*

AI Readiness

M7

Innovation Caucus Cards

Row 1 (Configuration cards – yellow)

Card	Question	Tags
1	How do your customers pay for your products/processes/services?	CONFIGURATION · TRANSACTIONS
2	How are your skills, capabilities and resources aligned to your revenue model(s)?	CONFIGURATION · STRUCTURE
3	What, if any, other businesses is your business dependent upon?	CONFIGURATION · NETWORK
4	What are the main products/processes/services that your customers use in conjunction with your offering?	CONFIGURATION · NETWORK
5	What is the main competitive advantage of your business model (offering, experience, configuration)?	CONFIGURATION · REVENUE MODEL
6	How can your business modularise (i.e. reduce to different parts) your product/process/service?	CONFIGURATION · TRANSACTIONS
7	Where, when and how can there be other transactions with customers?	CONFIGURATION · TRANSACTIONS

Row 2 (Configuration cards)

Card	Question	Tags
1	How can your business better align your skills and resources for growth?	CONFIGURATION · STRUCTURE
2	How can your business handle multiple business models?	CONFIGURATION · STRUCTURE
3	How can the dependence of your business on other products/processes/services be reduced?	CONFIGURATION · NETWORK
4	How can you increase the dependence of other businesses on your product/process/service?	CONFIGURATION · NETWORK
5	What can your business offer that no one else can (i.e. are your products/processes/services unique)?	CONFIGURATION · REVENUE MODEL
6	How can your product/process/service be reconfigured to create a new offering?	CONFIGURATION · REVENUE MODEL
7	How can your business get customers to pay more?	CONFIGURATION · REVENUE MODEL

Row 3

Card	Question	Tags
1	How can your business grow the customer base?	CONFIGURATION · REVENUE MODEL
2	How can your business reduce the costs of growth?	CONFIGURATION · REVENUE MODEL
3	Describe in what areas you think AI technologies could augment professional expertise	IMAGINING AI
4	Identify what tasks could be enhanced or enabled with the use of AI technologies	IMAGINING AI
5	Describe new clients and markets that could be identified and accessed using AI technologies	IMAGINING AI
6	Describe what tasks or workflows in your firm could be automated with AI technologies	IMAGINING AI
7	Identify what processes in your firm could be optimised with AI technologies service(s)	IMAGINING AI

Row 4

Card	Question	Tags
1	Identify new services your firm would develop based on AI technologies	IMAGINING AI
2	Identify what judgements or decision making could be enhanced with AI technologies	IMAGINING AI
3	Describe which of your services could be augmented by AI technologies to provide greater accuracy	IMAGINING AI
4	Is there scope to consider a more substantive change to the business model?	PIVOT
5	Is there scope to consider a more substantive change to the business model?	PIVOT
6	Is it time to pause and rethink the business model?	STOP
7	Is it time to pause and rethink the business model?	STOP

Image: Antoine-Rault Unsplash

Template: The Innovation Roadmap

Business Model Innovation Roadmap

1
Innovation Opportunity

Select 1 business model innovation card that you regard as the most relevant to you

NOW GO TO 2

3
Change Required

What has to change in your firm for the outcome / vision described in **2** to work

4
Organisational Challenges

What are the major challenges and/or risks associated with realising the outcome/vision and changes described in **2** and **3**?

5
Stakeholder Engagement

Briefly describe who you know and/or would need to engage (internally or externally) to achieve **2** and **3** and overcome **4**

6
Resources Required

Briefly describe what resources you have or would need to achieve **2** and **3** and overcome **4**

2
Business Outcome

Briefly describe what you consider a positive outcome to look like in relation to the selected card in **1**

Place business model innovation card here

Beneficiary/ beneficiaries

Place persona card here

Key changes required may include:

- Organizational culture
- Business processes
- Ways of working
- Investment model
- Billing model

Key challenges to consider may include:

- Leadership buy-in
- Resources
- Capabilities
- Revenue model
- Careers

Key individuals to consider may include:

- Firm leaders
- Innovation Managers
- Practice are leads
- Clients
- Regulators
- Tech providers

Key resources to consider

- Time
- Investment
- Expertise

Key points to consider:

- How does the business benefit?
- How do clients benefit?
- How do partners benefit?

M8 Define the innovation beneficiaries

1. Purpose
To define the beneficiaries of the AI-enabled innovation and the outcomes for them.

2. Duration
30 to 50 minutes.

3. What you need
Persona template (if you want to create your own personas) and time and expertise to create your own set of personas. OR Persona set included in the toolkit.

4. How to prepare
Produce a persona set relevant to your firm and sector. Review the persona template provided and adjust if needed. Get together a small team from across the organisation, and spend an hour filling out the templates so that you have a set of about 8 to 10 personas, spread across your organisation and client organisations. OR Review the persona set provided. This includes a brief summary of the key challenges or issues facing the persona in their professional role. Does it fit with roles and terminology used in your organisation or sector? Edit and adapt as required. Add any missing personas relevant to your firm or sector using the same format.

5. How to run this activity
First review the persona set you have decided to use (either the one included in this toolkit or one you have created). Invite feedback from colleagues who know the firm and the sector well, asking them to highlight anything that concerns them. Discuss which of these personas you want to focus on in your exploration of AI. Who do you think would benefit most from the innovation you discussed earlier? While any professional services firm is clearly trying to achieve outcomes for clients, can you drill down to define more precisely what you think the potential benefits might be for clients that address concerns or issues they have? Alternatively, are there barriers or issues in the firm faced by employees that this potential innovation could address? When you have discussed a range of potential beneficiaries, pick one to focus on in the sprint and specify the intended outcome for them using this format:

> **This innovation will help…… [persona] to achieve…… [action/behaviour] which is related to…… [ultimate business goal].**

Place the target beneficiary on the box in the **M7** Innovation Roadmap. This will allow you to maintain a focus on the target beneficiary of the AI innovation you selected in activity **M7**.

6. Output
A set of personas, including one target AI beneficiary, relevant to your firm and sector that is recognisable to participants in the sprint but open enough for them to feel they can add to or adapt.

7. Outcome
- A shared focus on who the potential beneficiaries of innovation might be and their everyday worlds and concerns
- A shared prioritisation of the key beneficiaries you will focus on in the sprint and the potential outcomes for them.

8. Background
One of the benefits of using a 'design thinking' or 'service design' approach that's often cited is that it brings a focus on the 'user'. Frequently this takes the form of creating a set of 'personas', mini-profiles based on composites of real people. This can help a design team anchor their idea generation and development through the lens of the people who will experience the new service. Sometimes personas are created on the basis of research, often qualitative (for example interviews) and sometimes quantitative. While personas can be helpful, there is a danger of unconscious bias in creating and using them. To minimise this risk, involve a diverse group of people in creating and reviewing the personas and

ask them to help with the collective effort of mapping the individuals who might be beneficiaries of innovation, while at the same time bringing to life principles of equality, inclusivity and diversity.

In the case of professional services firms, the beneficiaries of innovation may be a wide range of people, including stakeholders inside professional firms or client organisations who are not directly involved in delivering the service. The approach we propose is to explore and define the potential beneficiaries of AI, drawing on your knowledge of your staff, clients, partners, sub-contractors and other key stakeholders such as regulators. To do this you will review a list of potential beneficiaries provided which was developed for use with professional services firms, or you can use a blank template provided to create your own set of personas relevant to your firm or sector.

Image: Bruno Thethe on Pexels

Template: Personas (internal and external)

Client Employee

Organisation type or sector _ _ _ _ _ _ _ _
_ _
Name _
Age _
Role _
Experience level _ _ _ _ _ _ _ _ _ _ _ _ _ _

About the organisation
What are they trying to achieve?

Willingness to learn / experiment
Low — Medium — High

Desire to be seen as an innovator
Low — Medium — High

Involvement in governance of data-sharing
Low — Medium — High

What are they trying to achieve?
Long term and short term

Personal | Work

Techonology Expertise / Usage

Personal | Work

Firm Employee

Name _
Age _
Role _
Practical area _ _ _ _ _ _ _ _ _ _ _ _ _ _ _ _
Experience level _ _ _ _ _ _ _ _ _ _ _ _ _ _

About the organisation
What are they trying to achieve?

Willingness to learn / experiment
Low — Medium — High

Attachment to professional autonomy
Low — Medium — High

Involvement in governance of change in firm
Low — Medium — High

What are they trying to achieve?
Long term and short term

Personal | Work

Techonology Expertise / Usage

Personal | Work

Describe the relationship between the professional services firm and its clients

Tool: Pre-defined persona cards

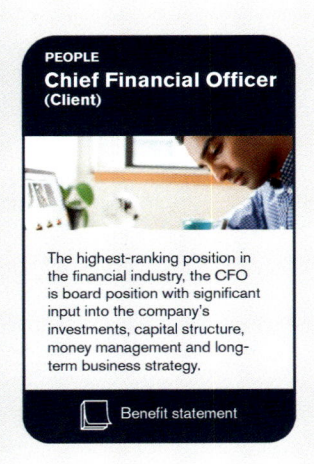

PEOPLE — Partner
Part owner of the firm, responsible for a practice areas and team to deliver expert services to client base.
Benefit statement

PEOPLE — Senior Partner
Firm ambassador, supporting most valued clients and leader of governance / strategic oversight.
Benefit statement

PEOPLE — Managing Partner
Member of firm partnership with day to day responsibility for running of the business.
Benefit statement

PEOPLE — Chief Financial Officer (Client)
The highest-ranking position in the financial industry, the CFO is board position with significant input into the company's investments, capital structure, money management and long-term business strategy.
Benefit statement

PEOPLE — General Council (Client)
The internal 'chief lawyer' in a client, the GC The General Council is a C-level executive who provides legal advice and acts as a legal representative for the company.
Benefit statement

PEOPLE (Accounting sector) — Director / Senior manager
Experienced fee-earner supporting partners in the delivery of services to clients, including some internal operational responsibilities.
Benefit statement

PEOPLE (Law sector) — Senior Associate / Associate
Experienced fee-earner supporting partners in the delivery of services to clients, including some internal operational responsibilities.
Benefit statement

PEOPLE — Business Development Manager
Responsible for identifying targets, general leads, building and maintaining relationships, gathering and sharing business intelligence within the firm.
Benefit statement

PEOPLE — Business Owner
Wears multiple hats covering all business functions, juggling responsibilities and making decisions.
Benefit statement

PEOPLE — Professional in Client Organisation
Part of the client's operations, with different levels of experience in terms of working with external professionals.
Benefit statement

M9 Rapid idea generation

1. Purpose
To involve participants in generating many ideas in a short space of time from a wide variety of perspectives.

2. Duration
10 minutes.

3. What you need
All participants need a piece of A4 or A3 paper and a pencil or pen. If running this remotely, we recommend sticking with pen and paper (the tactile element contributes to the idea generation) and then asking participants to photograph their sheets with their smartphones and upload the images to a shared location.

4. How to prepare
- Define the challenge statement you will use for this activity, which might be a variant of or an aspect of the challenge statement for your whole design sprint. For example, "How can we make better use of our data to deliver targeted solutions to our clients?"
- Decide on the questions you want to ask - see the suggestions below. Adapt them to the cultural context you are working within so that participants will be immediately familiar with the references. Ensure you have a mix of about eight individuals (both real and fictional, contemporary and historic) and organisations of different times including governments, corporate firms, retailers, SMEs as well as activists and movements.

5. How to run this activity
Explain the exercise. Get participants ready with their paper and pen. They can use blank paper or paper folded up into eight rectangles. Remind them of the challenge question they will respond to. Call out one question at a time. Ask participants to quickly write down or sketch their ideas to each question on the paper. Give them about 45 seconds per question.

Repeat this, seven more times. Then, ask participants to share their ideas (in plenary or in small groups). Are there any common themes? What's the most unviable? While some of the ideas may be ridiculous or problematic, are there any nuggets in these ideas that you can build on?

Example questions: Ask participants, "if the following were to address this challenge…": (See opposite)

6. Output
Sheets with rapidly sketched or written ideas. If working remotely, remember to ask participants to take and upload photos of their finished sheets.

7. Outcome
The result of using this method is that across the group of participants, a broad range of ideas will have been generated.

8. Background
There are many different ways of generating ideas; this one is a quick-fire exercise that gets participants to come up with many ideas in a short space of time, generating possible solutions to the challenge from the perspective of others. This exercise will prompt people to think outside their usual frames of reference. Although some of the ideas will be implausible or ethically problematic, the activity of generating and discussing them may help participants challenge their own assumptions and open up to new possibilities.

What would Google do?

What would a premium retailer such as Waitrose/John Lewis Partnership do?

What would a price conscious high street retailer do?

What would Apple do?

What would a platform that connects people with resources for hire, e.g., Airbnb, do?

What would China do?

What would a small Scandinavian country do?

What would Trump do?

What would a criminal gang do?

What would a social movement inspired by Gandhi do?

What would Harry Potter do?

What would Elon Musk do?

What would an activist group like Extinction Rebellion do?

Image: Fauxels on Pexels

M10 Make and review models and mock-ups

1. Purpose
Bring ideas to life, share them and surface assumptions and differences of opinion.

2. Duration
- 30 minutes minimum (for making)
- 5 minutes per group (for sharing).

3. What you need
- Clean model-making materials (see list below)
- Small toys, e.g., Lego people can be useful
- Scissors
- Fixing materials, e.g., tape, glue, glue dots.

4. How to prepare
Gather the materials you will need on a side table that all participants can access if co-located. If working remotely, you could invite participants in advance to gather these or equivalent, easily available materials in preparation for the sprint. Emphasise that they should use cheap and recyclable products. It is best to retain the physical making element of this method, but if absolutely necessary there are online tools that could provide an approximation of the experience.

5. How to run this activity
Explain the purpose of the activity and encourage people to work in ways that they don't usually do and may not feel comfortable with. Ask people to put themselves in the shoes of your personas. For example, tell them to imagine a moment in the future professional service in which the beneficiaries or users are interacting – which could be digital or face to face – in which AI is involved in some way.

Ask them to use the materials provided, or that they have to hand at their location, to mock-up this future interaction between the beneficiary/beneficiaries and the innovation. Talk them through the materials you have provided or ask remote participants to do a very quick 'show and tell' of the materials they have gathered.

As the teams start working, go round each group, observe what they are doing, and ask for clarification. Remind each group to define how the user or beneficiary they selected will experience the interaction which is associated with the innovation and enabled by AI. At the end of the session each group should share their model with the wider group to obtain feedback. This should include defining who is the user/beneficiary; how they interact with the AI-enabled professional service; and what's the outcome for them.

6. Output
Models made of recyclable materials (remember to photograph them, or invite remote participants to upload their photos, before recycling!). See list on next page.

7. Outcome
A shift from the mostly abstract and conceptual designing of the previous tools and methods to a more embodied process that promotes a strong sense of involvement (and fun) among participants.

8. Background
The principles and practices of prototyping are now built into how many organisations develop products and services including those using 'design thinking, 'agile' and 'lean start-up'. Associated with technology product development, the activity of making models is built into many creative practices including design, architecture, fashion and the arts. The basic idea is that making and reviewing models (also referred to as mock-ups) can bring participants' ideas to life. This enables a wider group of people, either in the workshop, or afterwards, to understand what the proposed service or change would be like from the perspective of its users or beneficiaries. This helps to surface different understandings of the potential solution, as well as the challenge it responds to. These mock-ups can be made of nearly anything, such as recyclable 3D materials as well as paper for people to cut out and stick together. It's important when using this method in professional services to give people permission to bring their ideas to life. Participants usually enjoy using their craft skills, no matter how rudimentary.

Example: Models and mock-ups from a professional services firm design sprint.

Model-Making Materials List

In order to get the most from the exercise of creating models and mock-ups we suggest using the following:

- **Cardboard boxes of varying sizes**
- **Empty packaging boxes, cereal packets, containers, etc.**
- **Plastic (e.g., bubble wrap, sheets, bags) preferably clear, although it's possible to use coloured**
- **A4 and A3 white paper (printer paper is ideal) and envelopes**
- **Card of varied colour and thickness**
- **Newspapers, magazines, brochures and leaflets**
- **Tissue and/or wrapping paper**
- **White or coloured napkins, paper cups and plates**
- **Wooden or plastic cutlery**
- **Fabric or cloth scraps.**

Note:
- **Ensure recyclable materials are clean and dry**
- **Do not use anything containing sensitive data**
- **Participants working remotely need smaller quantities.**

M11 Storyboarding

1. Purpose
To enable participants to detail and share their potential innovation in the professional services context, in an accessible format that communicates the lived experience of the beneficiary or user.

2. Duration
30 minutes.

3. What you need
- **M11** Visual Icon Library for participants to cut up or work with digitally
- **M11** Storyboard Template
- Coloured pens, scissors, glue and old magazines and newspapers to cut up
- Stickers.

4. How to prepare
Ensure your participants have their Innovation Roadmap to hand, identifying the beneficiary and outcome.

5. How to run this activity
Provide participants with the Storyboard Template and Visual Icon Library. These can easily be shared as digital images. The template can be printed out at home for draft sketching, and a shared editable version uploaded on Mural, Miro or similar collaborative web tool. Similarly, the icons in the Visual Icon Library are available as individual digital files. Their storyboards can include imagery from the icon library, or cut out from magazines, or written in by participants, or all three. Brief participants so they have a clear focus on creating a story, visually and collaboratively, to communicate something about the future AI-enabled professional service or firm. Ask participants to share their storyboards, in the room or via screen share on your collaborative meetings platform, explaining in particular who the user or beneficiary is, what they experience and the outcome.

6. Output
A set of stories in a visually engaging format.

7. Outcome
As with the Future Artefacts and Persona Templates, visual representations help to make proposed innovations feel more real to participants, and therefore easier to implement.

8. Background
Creating and discussing a storyboard is a good way to synthesise and communicate ideas. A simple way to think of a storyboard is as a sequence of frames, as in a comic book. This exercise asks participants to work collaboratively in small groups to construct an illustrated storyboard that communicates key aspects of the AI-enabled innovation. Doing this can help participants connect and bring together their insights from different elements of the sprint; understandings of the challenge or problem, perspectives on opportunities presented by AI technologies, a sense of the experience of beneficiaries and the overall outcomes. Reviewing and discussing a storyboard with colleagues will generate insights into the challenges of implementation. It's not intended to be a final design for how an AI-service should work in practice. Instead, creating and discussing a series of storyboards allows participants from across the firm to build and refine a shared understanding of the potential for AI for their organisation, as well as surfacing some assumptions.

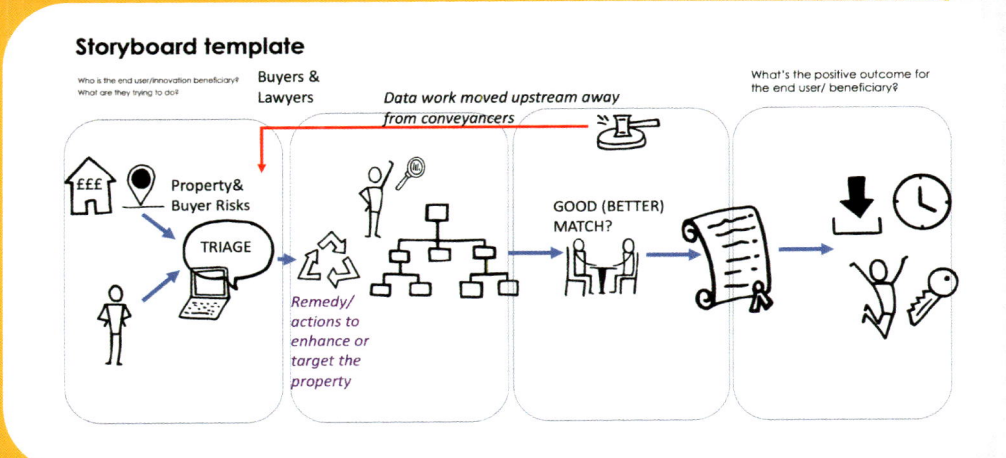

Example: Completed Storyboard Template created using shared whiteboard function on Zoom. Text has been replaced to protect confidential content.

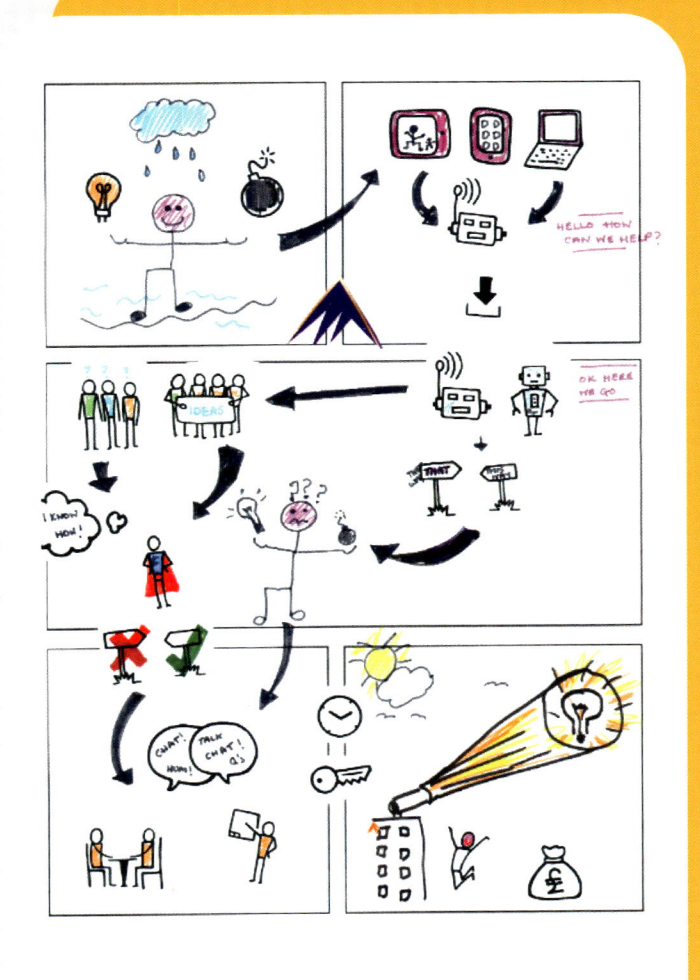

Example: Completed Storyboard Template from in-person design sprint.

AI Readiness

M12

Storyboarding Icon Library

M12 Get 360-degree feedback

1. Purpose
To scrutinise early-stage ideas from multiple perspectives in order to improve them.

2. Duration
20 to 45 minutes depending on the number of teams.

3. What you need
- Time and space
- A timekeeper to manage the flow of presentations and feedback
- Someone to record the feedback, in note form, audio, video, or a combination.
- People with different perspectives who can stand in for clients, partners, stakeholders and staff in business support functions and so on, so you can get 360-degree perspectives on the developing ideas.

4. How to prepare
Ensure teams who are going to share their ideas have a clear framework (such as the one suggested below) and enough time to prepare.

5. How to run this activity
First, set expectations about the behaviours and kinds of feedback you expect from participants. Ask them to be positive and critical — it will help the other team if you ask challenging questions. After each presentation, invite questions and feedback from participants. Ensure that teams have time to reflect on the feedback they received, work again on their ideas, and know when they have to produce their final versions and in what format.

6. Outputs
- Revised concepts
- Notes or other documentation from feedback.

7. Outcome
The result of going through a round of presentations and feedback will be a sense of the opportunities shared across the participants and teams. Having been exposed to critical feedback, the ideas can be improved through a further cycle of work.

8. Background
Prototyping is central to the design process. Designers make a mock-up or model which communicates an aspect of the concept they have developed as a potential solution or response to the issue they are exploring. Doing a version of prototyping allows you to share and get feedback on your ideas at an early stage, so that you can develop and refine them or reject them and move on. Be aware of solution fixation, where a team has become so attached to a concept that they can't hear feedback. Prototyping is never final, and is cyclical; exploring early-stage, partial responses or solutions allows a team to continue to develop their understanding of the problem or issue. Other professions have similar practices; for example, sharing a draft text or document which is then changed as a result of the feedback received. Prototyping has three specific attributes:
- Giving physical form to ideas; using objects and imagery (and possibly role play) to bring ideas to life in ways that allow many forms of interpretation
- Creating a mock-up or model to show how the target beneficiary or end user would experience a change or innovation
- Maintaining a focus on how the concept would work in practice, e.g., how the new interface or service touchpoint would be used in everyday situations.

M13 Complete the innovation roadmap

1. Purpose
To finalise your innovation roadmap as a shared understanding of the AI enabled innovation in your firm.

2. Duration
45 minutes.

3. What you need
- Your incomplete **M7** Innovation Roadmap template
- Read section 3.5, 'Approaches to the deployment of AI in accounting and law firms in England' which provides six different approaches to how professional services firms might develop towards AI readiness.

4. How to prepare
Ask participants to read section 3.5 before the session.

5. How to run this activity
Invite participants to discuss their initial responses to the section:
- Which approaches seem most relevant to your firm/sector? Why?
- What would be the impact on your firm if you adopted one of these approaches?
- What resources and capabilities would such an approach demand?
- Who within the firm will be most affected, and how? How will the approach impact relations with clients, strategic partner firms and regulators?

Take the insights generated and ask the team to think about how your firm might have to adapt. Review your incomplete Innovation Roadmap and turn to the boxes that have not yet been completed. These include questions and prompts to help you think about different aspects of implementation:

- Box 3: What has to change in your firm for the outcome or vision in Box 2 to work?
- Box 4: What are the major challenges and/or risks associated with realising the outcome or vision and changes described in Boxes 2 and 3?
- Box 5: Describe who you know and/or would need to engage, internally or externally, to secure the Box 2 outcome, achieve the change(s) required by Box 3 and overcome the organisational challenges in Box 4.
- Box 6: Describe the resources you have or would need in order to achieve the Box 2 vision and the change(s) required by Box 3 and overcome the challenges in Box 4.

Complete each box in as much detail as you can. The roadmap will serve as a blueprint for the implementation of your solution and will assist you in identifying next steps.

6. Output
Completed **M7** Innovation Roadmap.

7. Outcome
A shared understanding of the potential innovation, the intended outcome, the changes required, the implementation challenges and resources required.

8. Background
In **M7** 'Start the Innovation Roadmap' you were asked to select one or more business model innovation cards, and to complete the last box (Box 2) only. Now that you have developed your AI solution and considered a wide range of issues, you can consider the potential challenges and risks associated with implementing it within your firm, as well as whom you may need to involve and what resources are required (Boxes 3–6).

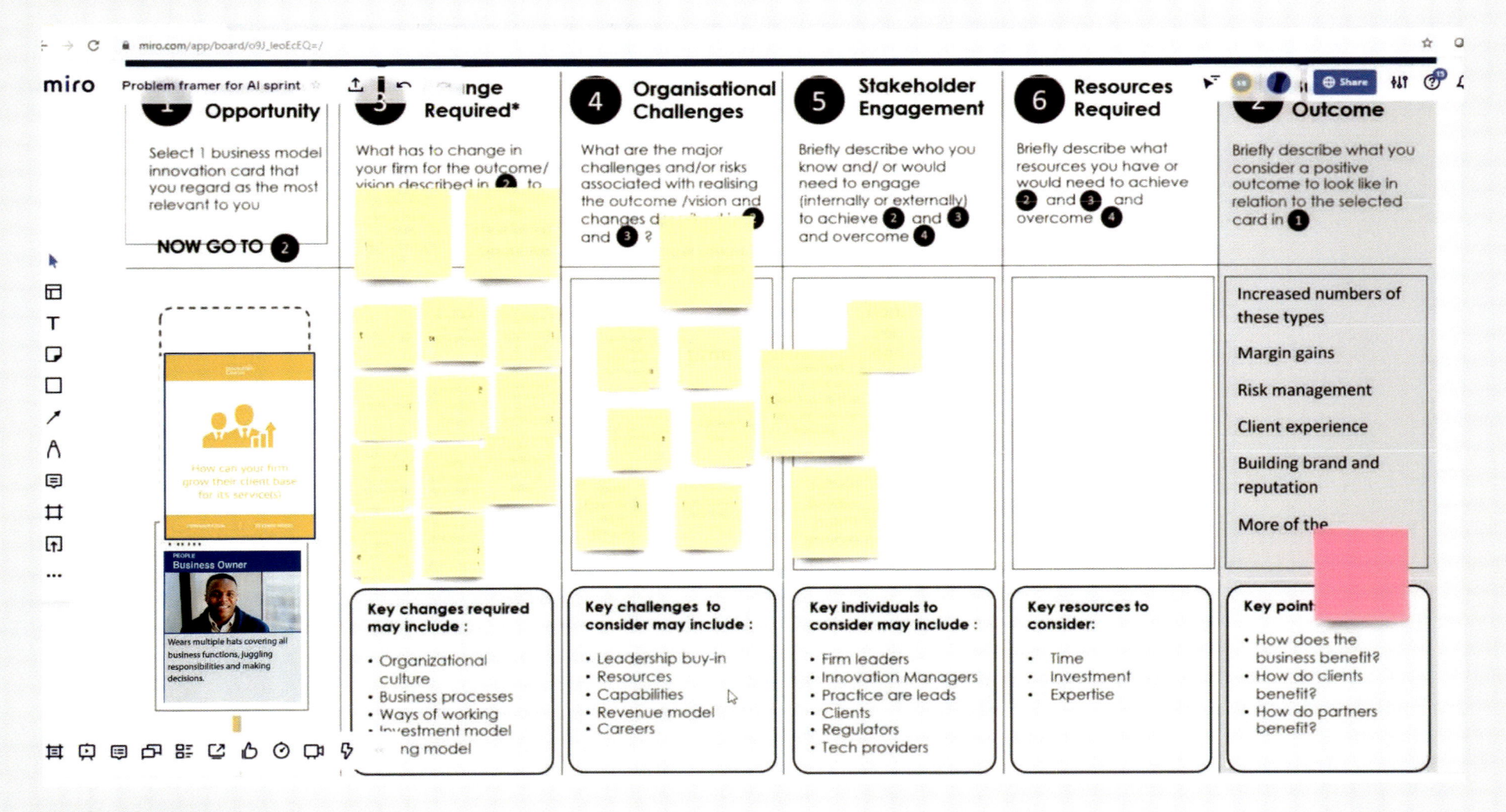

Example: Innovation Roadmap near completion. From an online sprint using Miro. Text has been obscured to protect confidential content.

M14 Make Presentations and share feedback

1. Purpose
To present ideas developed in the design phase of the sprint, articulate the proposed innovation and get feedback to further improve the ideas.

2. Duration
75 minutes.

3. What you need
Groups may wish to prepare visual content or use material developed during the sprint, such as the M11 Storyboarding templates or models, but this is optional.

4. How to prepare
Groups discuss their presentations in advance. Some basic guidelines on presenting and giving feedback are helpful:
- Remember to allow for differences in presenting methods if some or all groups are working remotely and presenting via an online platform
- Develop a framework for people to present to and brief teams on it
- Develop a framework for giving feedback and brief teams on it.

The criteria for assessing a proposal will depend on the aims of your AI readiness sprint. Some suggested questions to help you critically assess each proposal are these:

Originality
- To what extend does this proposal invite you to rethink the business of the firm, or your professional practice?
- To what extent does this proposal create new forms of value?

Effectiveness
- To what extent would the proposal make the firm more effective in delivering value to clients?

Efficiency
- To what extent would the proposal make the firm more efficient in delivering value to clients?

Feasibility
- What would be required for this proposal to be brought to life?
- Are the identified barriers or changes the relevant ones?
- What's missing from descriptions of the implementation issues presented?

Assumptions
- What assumptions are being made?
- What might be the unintended consequences of these proposals?
- What blind spots do the presentations reveal?

5. How to run this activity

Brief the groups on the importance of keeping to the allocated timing; if they over-run it will reduce the time for, and probably the quality of, feedback from colleagues. Invite short presentations from each group, ideally a maximum of 10 minutes per group, based on a structure they have been briefed for in advance, such as:
- What is the problem/challenge/opportunity in terms of the business model? (1 min)
- What is the AI capability you want to employ to address this? (1 min)
- What is the business model innovation that will be achieved (i.e., what outcome will it lead to or enhance) and who will be the beneficiary(ies)? (2 mins)
- What will change and for whom? Show your model or storyboard to communicate how things change for your persona(s) (3 mins)
- What are the issues and barriers in implementing this? (3 mins)

Make suggestions to the groups about how best to present their ideas, which might sound obvious but are often overlooked in the business and excitement of the overall process:
- How clear are you in your own mind about what you're presenting?
- Will everyone understand references/idioms/jargon etc?
- If you're using visual materials will they be fully visible (especially if working remotely)?

Similarly, it's worth making suggestions to those giving feedback:
- Don't be judgmental, be curious; receiving feedback isn't always easy
- Can you build on the material presented rather than knock it down? (Try saying "Yes, and…" instead of "Yes, but…" or just "No!")
- Does the presentation link with, or cause you to think differently about your own ideas? And so on.

6. Outputs

Greater clarity about ideas for AI and/or business model innovation, and insights generated from feedback.

7. Outcomes

A stronger commitment to innovation as a process and to specific ideas. Or, potentially, the realisation that an idea is not workable - which is itself a valid outcome. No design process only results in successful or viable ideas. The ideas that stay on the cutting room floor (as they say in the film industry) can provide the most valuable learning opportunities.

Image: JR Korpa on Unsplash

M15 So What? Now What?

1. Purpose
To surface different perspectives within the group on whether proposed innovations are aligned with the rationale for change, and to pre-empt any concerns that the design sprint won't lead to the necessary actions.

2. Duration
30 to 45 minutes.

3. What you need
Flipchart and Post-It notes to capture feedback (or digital equivalent).

4. How to prepare
Gather all participants and invite the sprint Sponsor, sprint Leader (if not already present) and other stakeholders who can add value at this stage. If you are running this remotely or as a hybrid, ensure that you have online collaboration tools that everyone can access.

5. How to run this activity
Run this activity with the whole group if there are up to about 12 people or split them into smaller groups with a minimum of four per group. Try to ensure that everyone speaks at least once during this activity. Frame the activity by asking participants just to think about the following questions for one minute:

- What just happened?
- What stood out for you?
- What, if anything, has changed in your view of AI readiness?

- Then invite participants to write down their responses to the following prompt on Post-It notes - or in the 'chat' function of whatever online meetings platform you are using for remote participants - for two minutes:
- So what?
- Why is this important?
- What patterns do you see in the process as a whole and its constituent parts?
- What does that tell you about your firm's potential for change?

Bring everyone together to share their thoughts by sticking their Post-It notes on the wall or writing on a shared virtual whiteboard. Ask the group to review all the points raised and suggest the four or five most salient. Capture these on the flipchart/virtual whiteboard. Return to individual work with the second prompt:
- Now what?
- What actions are sensible and achievable?
- What might happen if we don't act?

As before, share the Post-It notes or 'chat' comments and capture key points on the flipchart or virtual whiteboard.

6. Output
Post-It Notes, flipchart sheets, virtual whiteboard images, recorded discussion.

7. Outcome
Generates trust in the process and in the capability and willingness of the team to deliver on the ideas generated.

8. Background
This allows participants to voice their enthusiasm and inevitable concerns about both the collaborative design approach and about AI and business model innovation.

A 'mini' version, in which the two questions are discussed in one five- or six-minute hit, can be valuable after all or some of the preceding activities, to help ensure ongoing alignment with the sprint's purpose and with the toolkit section on 'Opportunities and challenges of AI readiness'. This method is adapted from Liberating Structures, a website with many exercises that are useful for managing change in organisations, particularly among professionals with a high degree of investment in their existing knowledge and expertise.

The exercises are made available under a Creative Commons license. See:

Liberating Structures
www.liberatingstructures.com

For more ideas about running this and similar exercises remotely, see:

Virtual Liberating Structures
https://dzone.com/articles/remote-agile-part-2-virtual-liberating-structures

AI Readiness

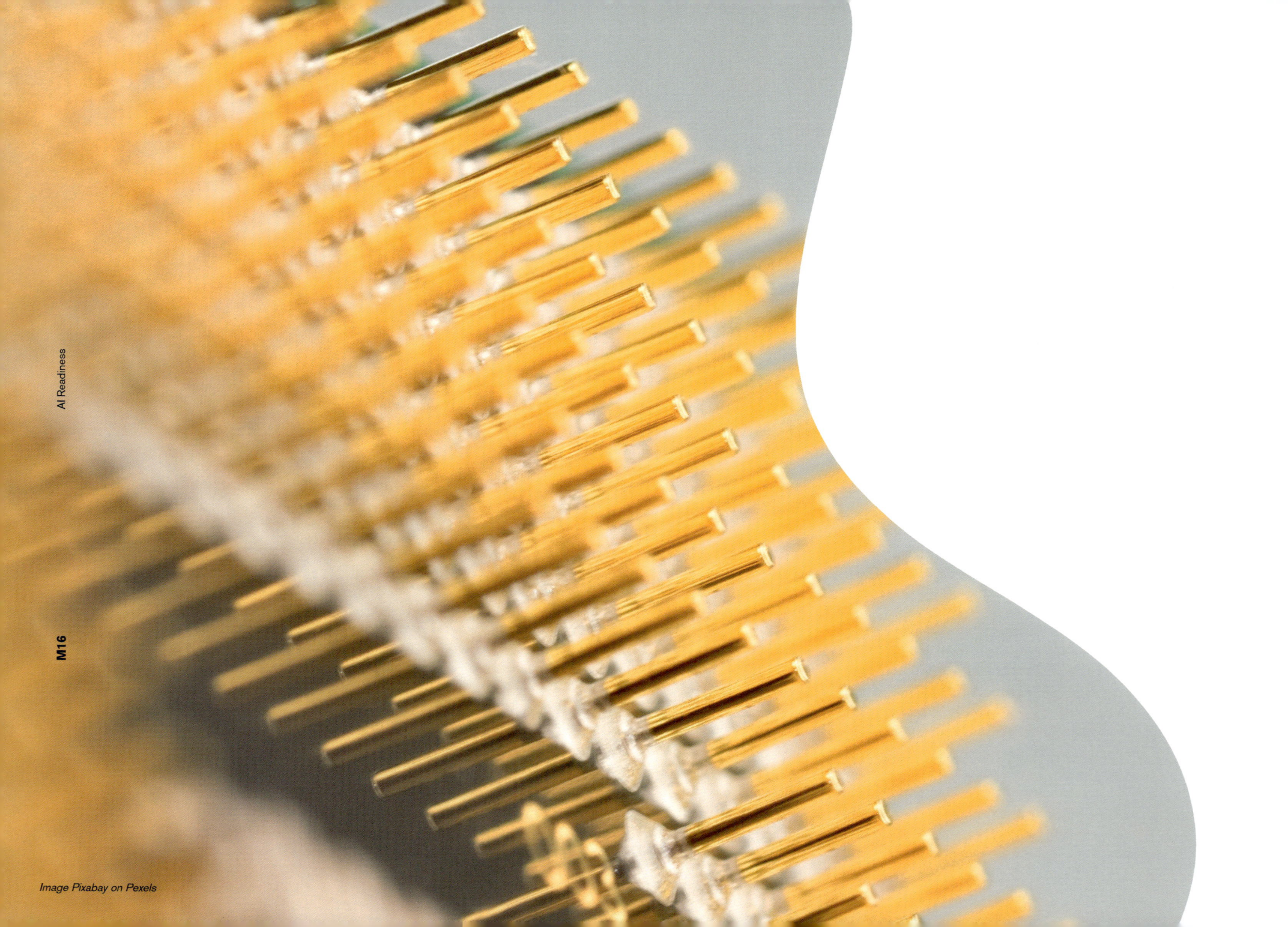

M16

Image Pixabay on Pexels

M16 Reflective conversation

1. Purpose
To generate insights about your ideas for innovation and about working with collaborative design methodologies.

2. Duration
30 to 45 minutes.

3. What you need
- Time and space
- Paper/pens or laptops etc.

4. How to prepare
Define the relevant questions or prompts you want people to respond to.

5. How to run this activity
Remind participants of the purpose of collective learning and the objectives you wanted your sprint to achieve. Ask them to make individual notes in response to the following questions and to share their notes in plenary:

- What are your three top insights from having done the design sprint?
- To what extent are the ideas reliant on AI and/or connected to business model change?
- What are the barriers to adoption of AI technologies?
- Would the adoption and implementation of AI possibly lead to increased discrimination or negative consequences for some groups? What might this mean for the firm's commitments to equality, diversity and inclusivity?
- What are the benefits of working in this way?
- What would/will you tell the Managing Partner?
- What do you want to take forward in your own area of work/practice?
- What have you got out of the sprint, that you think you would not have had access to from other types of meeting, discussion or workshop?

6. Output
Participants' individual notes (if they're willing to share) and notes from the plenary.

7. Outcome
Awareness of collective learning and a sense of shared achievement.

8. Background
One of the principles associated with learning is creating outputs that allow people to synthesise what they have learned. At school or university this might be achieved by asking students to write a report or essay. Depending on the specific objectives you have for your sprint, you will expect different 'learning outcomes' to be achieved for participants. During our research, we found that there were important differences in how people in professional services firms responded to the opportunities of AI and of using the design sprint approach to explore them. This activity supports you to have a collective discussion to generate insights about going on this journey with these concepts and tools.

3 Understanding the landscape

3. Understanding the landscape

3.1	**What's going on in the landscape for mid-size law and accounting firms**	**104**
3.2	**Opportunities and challenges of AI readiness**	**107**
3.2.1	Opportunities for AI readiness in law and accounting	**109**
3.2.2	Challenges of AI readiness in law and accounting	**110**
3.3	**Learning from practice**	**113**
3.4	**Current uses of AI in accounting and law firms in England**	**115**
3.4.1	Case 1: The accounting or law firm as software vendor	**116**
3.4.2	Case 2: The accounting or law firm as data analyser	**118**
3.4.3	Case 3: The accounting or law firm as process and project consultant	**120**
3.4.4	Case 4: The accounting or law firm as automated business	**122**
3.4.5	Case 5: The efficient law or accounting firm	**124**
3.4.6	Case 6: The (re)integrated law or accounting firm – capturing value	**126**
3.4.7	Case 7: The accounting or law firm as innovation lab	**128**
3.5	**Approaches to the deployment of AI in accounting and law firms in England**	**130**
3.5.1	Approach 1: Addressing the AI competency challenge	**131**
3.5.2	Approach 2: The adoption dilemma	**132**
3.5.3	Approach 3: Managing expectations	**135**
3.5.4	Approach 4: Who needs to use AI in the next generation professional services firm?	**136**
3.5.5	Approach 5: Managing the change to the professional career path	**138**
3.5.6	Approach 6: Organising digital and data driven professional services	**141**

3.1 What's going on in the landscape for mid-size law and accounting firms

Legal and accountancy professional services are significant sectors in the UK economy, with the legal services market estimated to be worth £35.1bn in 2018[51] and accountancy professional services contributing an estimate £21bn to UK GDP.[52] Beyond the numbers, these sectors are market-leading internationally and contribute to the UK's global reputation as a place that is good for business. As professional services, they are deemed to be 'old' in so far as the sectors contain "organisations employing professionals from long-ago established and state recognised professions".[53] Thus, the institutional landscape and norms within which accountancy and legal services firms operate is relevant to the adoption of AI and ensuing productivity gains.

On the face of it, there is much in common between the two sectors, such as being services in the knowledge economy requiring high degrees of training and personal judgment. The primary service is the exchange of time for money, with value attributed to professionals of higher status achieved through years of experience, specialisms and client relationships.

The majority of professional services firms are partnership business models, typically with limited liability. Full-service offerings dominate, and there is wide geographical coverage from single locations to national coverage and multi-national. There are points of significant difference too. The first, and most significant, difference is the degree of statutory protection and market shelters. For legal services, 'solicitor' remains a protected term, with areas of reserved activity that require an appropriately qualified person and are subject to regulation. There are other pathways to qualification for work within regulated domains, such as Chartered Legal Executive. On the other hand, 'accountant' is not a protected term in the same way, which means that there are different controls, protections and barriers to entry. That said, accounting professional services firms have largely been established on the back of audit practice, which is a highly regulated area. Similarly, insolvency, as another key offering, is regulated by license. The overall breadth of services is far broader than this, including many consultancy services lines that are relevant to supporting business operations.

In recent years, the degree of regulation has been a movable feast. At a high level, legal services have been on a general pathway towards more openness, with the specific aims of promoting innovation and competition. The Legal Services Act 2007[54] was a pivotal point in enabling alternative business structures. For example, some large firms, including Gateley, Knights and others, have become PLCs. Also, the rise of alternative legal services providers can be traced back to this time and has opened the door for many of the large accountancy practices to create legal services departments and challenge incumbents. In this regard the lines between the two sectors have blurred and continue to do so. The Competition and Markets Authority has been an important actor in driving price transparency and quality in the last five years or so, maintaining a monitoring eye on consumer engagement in the legal sector.[55]

Conversely, audit has been subject to pressure for more regulation and regulatory reform, particularly following high-profile corporate collapses like BHS and Carillion.

Image: August de Richelieu on Pexels

Public investigations such as the Brydon Review into the Quality and Effectiveness of Audit[56] and the Kingman Review of the Financial Reporting Council[57] are influencing the direction of this reform. Such reforms, for both accountancy and legal services, are significant for how AI technologies align with stakeholder interests, and in ensuring the primary function of protecting the public is at the core of AI readiness. Other observations and factors relevant to technology-led disruption:

- The variety among professional bodies and how that influences sector leadership on these issues. Accountancy has a high degree of fragmentation for similarly qualified professionals by comparison with law yet appears to have greater ability to transcend boundaries through adoption of codes and standards compared to the tight jurisdictions governing the rule of law.
- The degree of separation between the regulatory function and professional bodies/membership offerings.

There are many more legal firms in the UK than accountancy professional services practices, but the scale of the firms at the top of the accountancy market dwarfs the largest equivalents in legal services. There is a very significant gap in resources between the 'Big Four' firms and the next tier in accountancy.

Finally, beyond the firms, regulation and professional bodies, there are several other institutions that affect AI readiness, whether directly or indirectly, such as government bodies including Companies House, HMRC, Department of Business, Energy and Industrial Strategy (BEIS) and Department of Culture, Media and Sport (DCMS), amongst others. BEIS and DCMS are closer to the strategic side of business engagement and policy making, whereas Companies House and HMRC are closer to implementation, driving agendas such as the Making Tax Digital campaign that requires digital transformation of many clients' accounts and contributes to a firm's readiness to adopt AI.

Beyond government, there are numerous networks, trade organisations and media outlets that provide opportunities for peer networking, dissemination and knowledge exchange in support of ambitions such as AI readiness. For example, The Managing Partners Forum and TheCityUK are representative bodies based on a membership offering and Legal Geek is a media-based outlet running conferences and content related to legal services technology.

51 IRN Research (2019).
52 Oxford Economics (2018).
53 Faulconbridge and Muzio (2017).
54 Legal Services Act (2007).
55 Competition and Markets Authority (2016).
56 Brydon (2019).
57 Kingman (2018).

Image: Brett Sayles on Pexels

3.2 Opportunities and challenges of AI readiness

Artificial intelligence, with machine learning as an underpinning technology, has proved extremely successful in various domains including speech recognition, object detection in images, text classification, machine translation, genomics and autonomous vehicles. This provides the opportunity for existing businesses to make use of AI based technology to reduce costs, increase profits and develop and test new products more efficiently.[58] Much has been made of the potential applications of AI in professional service firms given the large amounts of data that have become available, although the reality of how the technology is being adopted and applied does not yet reflect the hype. However, AI technologies have significant potential to transform professional service firms, and while their adoption is improving quickly the impact is likely to be varied by sector, firm and function. While the professional services sector has hitherto been rather conservative in its approach to technology adoption, developments in AI, coupled with the rise of 'legal tech' and increasingly tech-savvy clients demanding better and faster services, have not only created pressure to adopt AI but also significant opportunities. There is now a range of narrow AI-enabled technologies in professional services that bring new capabilities to augment human expertise, particularly around the decision-making process which is central to professional practice. AI based tools, such as natural language processing, are already changing a range of practices, from discovery processes to contract review and prediction.[59] For example, lawyers now spend less than five per cent of their time on basic document review, as machine learning tools such as natural language processing are enabling e-discovery, thereby reducing the need for traditionally labour-intensive processes.

[58] Dang (2019).
[59] Alarie et al. (2018).

AI Readiness

3.2.1

Image: Johannes Plenio on Pexels

3.2.1 Opportunities for AI readiness in law and accounting

The opportunities in legal and accounting services largely revolve around three types of tools; logic-based tools used for knowledge representation and problem-solving, machine learning tools that allow computers to learn from data, and search and optimisation tools that allow intelligent search with many possible solutions. These AI based tools, in turn, open up a range of opportunities:

- Reducing costs by automating trivial tasks (e.g., customer service could be provided by dialogue systems)
- Assisting humans in decision making (e.g., resource allocation, profit forecast, etc.)
- Developing and testing new products more efficiently; And adding value to end-users (e.g., via tailored recommendations, insights, etc.).

General opportunities for both legal and accounting services include tools such as voice recognition and chat bots. Applications of AI in the legal services domain specifically include tasks such as legal citation resolution, case outcome analysis and prediction, models of legal reasoning and automatic contract generation and e-discovery, among other things.[60] The development of such tools could help automate tasks that now require a significant amount of time and labour. For example, repetitive contract generation could be automated by text generation systems underpinned by natural language processing and machine learning. Applications of AI in accounting and auditing include automating tasks such as document review, inventory counts, disclosure research, predictive risk analytics and client request lists.[61] Applying AI in accounting has great potential to support accountants with quick analysis of vast amounts of data.

[60] Katz (2012); Aletras et al. (2016); Aletras et al. (2019).

[61] Kokina and Davenport (2017); Sutton et al. (2016).

3.2.2 Challenges of AI readiness in law and accounting

The people challenge: Attitudes, social norms and AI adoption

One frequently discussed barrier to adoption of technical innovations in professional service firms concerns what is normally referred to as 'cultural resistance to change'. However, the concept of cultural resistance is often underspecified and, consequently, of little use in the elaboration of policy proposals for adoption of new technologies such as AI. Two main components of cultural barriers to adoption of innovation in professional service firms emerge. First, resistance to technical change can partly be attributed to the fact that professionals' expertise, skills and heuristics are tailored to the set of practices and routines shaped by the current technological paradigm. As such, innovations that are set to alter existing practices and routines also threaten the relevance of professional expertise and may require costly and time-consuming reskilling processes on the part of professionals. Second, professionals are individuals who strongly identify with their own occupation and are motivated to pursue occupational goals beyond economic incentives. In particular, professionals seek social recognition for their contribution to societal well-being by means of performing highly knowledge-intensive tasks. AI enabling technologies are set to strip some of those tasks from professionals and are, in part, perceived as undermining professional judgment. Hence, it is no surprise that negative attitudes towards AI enabling technologies emerge within the professions. These two components of 'resistance to change', also known as 'cultural-cognitive' and 'normative' pillars,[62] may partly explain the slow pace of adoption of AI within professional services and should be considered as a starting point in developing policy proposals aimed at inverting the trend.

However, how can the trend be reversed if professionals are so reluctant? In fact, forcing technical change against professionals' preferences and values may not be a smart move, even if feasible. In this respect, it's interesting to note that many professionals exhibit idiosyncratic preferences with respect to AI adoption. They are curious about emerging technologies and willing to experiment with them in order to change their workflow, improve their professional judgement and shape new practices and routines that can improve their firm's business model. These professionals, though, are often prevented from exploring and adopting technological capabilities by social norms that emerge in their firm or in their wider professional context. In particular, we observed that although many professionals are keen to experiment with AI tools, they form empirical and normative expectations that hinder their preferences for experimentation.

Empirical expectations are beliefs about what others do. In particular, professionals observe that most of their colleagues still operate in the context of the current technological paradigm and are reluctant to use AI tools. Normative expectations, on the other hand, are second-order beliefs about other people's attitudes. In particular, professionals believe that their colleagues believe that they should not be exploring or implementing AI tools in their practices and routines. Normative expectations are often accompanied by the anticipation of informal sanctions. Empirical and normative expectations shape the emergence and persistence of social norms[63] and invite convergence with patterns of behaviour that many individuals would not have followed in the absence of a norm. In the context of professional services firms, social norms shape convergence on practices and routines that discourage experimentation with and implementation of AI tools in a firm's operations.

Social norms, though, can be influenced in order to achieve a desired change. Three approaches in particular could prove useful. First, firms may try to counterbalance the anticipation of sanctions by attaching economic incentives to the use of AI tools; second, firms may try to change normative expectations by attaching value to technological development within the firm (e.g., by creating clear and ambitious career paths for professionals who choose to specialise in the development of technical tools aimed at improving a firm's operation); and third, firms may try to free professionals from norms, granting to each professional the possibility of finding their preferred workflow. Although attitudes and norms cannot entirely explain the slow pace of AI adoption within professional service firms, they constitute a pivotal aspect that must be taken into account when trying to shift business models towards AI readiness.

The following questions may be useful in assessing a firm's attitudes to change:

- What are the attitudes towards technology adoption in general, and AI adoption in particular, within your firm?
- Are these attitudes different at leadership, senior and junior levels?
- Do you support initiatives for technology adoption, particularly involving AI, within your firm?

The business model challenge

As discussed, AI technologies challenge the established business models in professional services, most of which are still based on limited liability partnership structures. One particular example is the legal services sector, where core business models based on partnership date back centuries and perpetuate traditional practice. Importantly, these can reinforce resistance to change and complicate the challenge of shifting attitudes and social norms. However, new technologies, such as those enabled by AI, promise to disrupt these business models fundamentally. For example, one of the business model components under threat is the revenue model, which in many subsectors is developed from billable hours. The automation of traditionally labour-intensive tasks, coupled with clients' changing expectations and growing demand for fixed fees, increasingly challenge the ability of professional service firms to use the billable hours model. This has implications not only for the profitability of firms, but also for how they are structured to create, deliver and capture value. The possibility of faster task completion using tools such as AI challenges the current partnership structure in which each partner has a big cohort of junior associates behind them, with partners carrying out more sophisticated work and juniors being assigned lower value work. Given that the latter often involves repetitive work that can be automated using new technologies, these structures are becoming unsustainable. The adoption of AI technologies will, in many cases, require a fundamental rethinking of service delivery, business practices and business models. This will involve reconfiguration and redeployment of resources no longer needed in impacted areas to new areas of service delivery that are augmented by the use of technology. As one study emphasises in the case of legal services, "the true benefits of artificially intelligent tools in the legal profession may be realized only once lawyers completely rethink the provision of legal services".[64] In this context, business model innovation is a valuable tool that can enable professional service firms to identify the business areas that are most prone to disruption, as well as where opportunities can be realised, and in the process reimagine service provision.

The data challenge

While professional services firms sit on a wealth of data that could be leveraged to create extra value for clients, there are a number of issues that can restrict firms' ability to extract value from that data, thereby creating additional barriers to technology adoption. While more technical in nature, these require consideration as part of any AI readiness journey. The issues include data security and the risk of data breaches, compounded by the fact that professional services firms hold confidential and commercially sensitive client information; General Data Protection Regulation (GDPR); cloud technology, since AI requires substantial data storage capability which brings its own challenges; and the often-unstructured nature of data. It may be desirable to consider hiring a data scientist among the technology capable legal staff required for building capability. However, there is a highly competitive market for data scientists across sectors, resulting in a shortage that is "becoming a serious constraint in some sectors".[65]

Professional services firms will need to follow technical developments in the use of AI and machine learning, such as the rapidly growing sophistication in data warehousing, in which requirements for both hardware and software are rapidly changing. In determining appropriate responses to these and related data challenges, firms should consider:
- What is the nature of the data?
- Who holds it and where is it stored?
- Who assesses and maintains quality and stability?
- How is the data accessed, and for what purposes?
- Who sets criteria and oversees the processes?
- What can go wrong?[66]

62 Scott (2008).
63 Bicchieri (2005).
64 Alarie et al. (2018) p. 123.
65 McAfee and Brynjolfsson (2012).
66 Adapted from National Academies of Sciences, Engineering, and Medicine (2018).

Type of use	Examples in Law	Examples in Accounting	Examples in Both
Practice management automation	Time-recording programs log hours spent in respect of each client.		Automatically generate invoices at the end of a relevant time period.
Predictive coding	Accesses thousands of documents to determine which ones are most relevant for purposes of disclosure. Reduces time spent on e-discovery and document review.		Ranks relevance of documents based on an initial training session.
Document assembly	Reads existing contracts and checks for missing clauses.		
Legal research/document review	Helps form a case strategy based on previous outcomes in similar cases.		
Voice recognition			Book appointments. Search documents
DIY and chatbots	Apply elements of document assembly to help individuals and businesses form their own legal documents. User access to basic legal assistance.	Resolve common queries from users such as when bills are due, latest account balance, and status on accounts.	
Analytics			Supports firms to focus their time on nuanced analysis. Data storytelling.
Code accounting entries		Improve accuracy of rule-based approaches, enabling greater automation of processes.	
Monthly or quarterly close procedure		Provides data from various sources then consolidates and merges it.	
Procurement		Track multiple supplier price changes.	
Accounts payable/receivable/ebilling		Learn the accounting code for the respective invoice thus support digital workflow, e.g. initiating payments and matching purchase orders.	
Audit			Digitalisation tracking; i.e. file accessed by whom and when.
Fraud detection		Pattern recognition of 'normal' activities, thus prediction of fraudulent activities.	
Automated data entry and data categorisation		Analyse broad financial trends.	
Natural language processing		Interpret contracts or deeds, i.e. extract key terms and compile and analyse information to perform risk assessments or other functions.	

Table 1: Examples of AI technology use in law and accounting

3.3 Learning from practice

Commentary on AI in business firms suggests that it presents many opportunities to enhance quality of work, for professionals and clients. However, there is lack of consensus around best practice and no single way of successfully implementing and adopting AI to achieve this. It is a major change for professional services firms, requiring suitable strategy, clear leadership, effective implementation and appropriate people management. The uses of AI in law and accounting vary in scope and ambition, ranging from simple automation to more complex prediction. Examples include practice management automation through time recording and automated invoice generation; predictive coding; document research; DIY/chatbots; fraud detection through data analytics and pattern recognition; interpreting contracts, leases and documents through natural language processing; automated data categorisation; automated appointment booking through voice recognition; document assembly (e.g., contract generation); e-discovery; case outcome analysis and prediction; and inventory count.

The following sections, covering accounting and law firms in England, first consider current uses of AI and then approaches to its deployment. They afford readers an opportunity to reflect on organisational and process realities within their firm and examine strategies that may help them identify an appropriate pathway to AI readiness. It focuses on understanding how companies use AI not only to solve existing business problems, but also to find new opportunities. The section on current uses of AI in accounting and law firms in England highlights practical applications of AI and demonstrates, through various examples, how firms utilise AI to improve performance, enhance efficiency and productivity, and transform their business to face future challenges. These cases highlight how AI is changing the way businesses operate at organisational level and how that might affect day-to-day professional work, how firm performance has been improved in various situations and the new business opportunities created. However, despite much discussion of the promise of AI and numerous success stories, many organisations fail in their AI implementation efforts. While appropriate AI tools and a workforce with adequate skills are important, it is equally important to overcome barriers arising from technological infrastructure, cultural factors such as resistance to change, strategic choices like becoming a technology provider, regulatory issues such as data capturing and sharing, and professional matters including recognising and incorporating new career paths. The section on approaches to the deployment of AI in accounting and law firms in England highlights how various organisations have implemented AI, overcoming the barriers to reap the rewards.

These two sections are neither comprehensive reviews nor are they commentaries on best practice. Rather, they highlight how some accounting and legal firms have taken various approaches to implement and adopt AI effectively. These examples are intended to contribute to discussion on AI in accounting and law, but not to be prescriptive. They provide some insight into why firms have invested in AI and how they have implemented it, as well as the impact on professionals, on how work is organised and on the firm as a whole. Table 1 sets out examples of how AI and related technologies are already being used, drawing on major reports published by relevant professional bodies[67] and commercial providers.[68]

---

67 Law Society (2018a); Law Society (2018b); ICAEW (2018); Ovaska-Few (2017).
68 Herbert Smith Freehills (2017); LawGeex (2019).

3.4 Current uses of AI in accounting and law firms in England

Image: Cottonbro on Pexels

The following cases provide a summary of insights from research into current uses of AI in accounting and law firms in England. The cases are anonymous and synthetic. They draw from multiple examples to illustrate the range of approaches and issues associated with different uses of AI.

The seven cases presented can be divided into three broad groups. First, innovations in business model. Cases of firms as software vendors, data analysers and process and project consultants reveal how AI can be used to change the client offering and extend it in new ways. Second, innovations in professional practice. Cases of the automated business, the efficient firm and the integrated firm reveal how AI can improve the way professional advice is generated, and value captured. Third, the case of firms as incubators. This considers ways in which law and accounting firms can engage with and develop technologies that meet their needs.

This section is designed to act as a stimulus for firms looking at how AI may be used as they develop their future business plans and consider the role of technology in changing both internal business processes and client offerings. Each case is relatively brief and provides an overview of the main features. The cases can also be used to inform bespoke design sprints if one or more seem relevant to future business plans.

3.4.1 Case 1: The accounting or law firm as software vendor

> "And then you come along and say… we're going to give you this tool, it means you're not going to give us work of this nature, but we'd like the work of that nature instead. And… by being ahead of the curve we're building trust with the client and saying actually we can save you money there, as a consequence we'd like more of the more interesting work. But it requires an education insight internally as well as one with the client."

Transforming the offering to clients

The law or accounting firm as software provider transforms the relationship between a firm and its clients. The current business model, based on accountants or lawyers from the firm solving a client's problem and advising them on a specific matter, remains in place. But the firm now also provides clients with access to software, powered by artificial intelligence, which allows straightforward accounting or legal processes to be completed without the involvement of the accounting or law firm. Software can also provide answers to basic accounting or legal questions. This means, for certain types of activity, the client does not need to interact with an accountant or lawyer from the firm; instead, they use the software provided by the accounting or law firm.

What can the software do?

The software, at the moment at least, can be used to complete the most straightforward processes that can be routinised (e.g., basic document production, basic book-keeping) and review work that involves the identification of simple and common structures and patterns (e.g., in legal services, document review for particular contract types). The software, therefore, potentially replaces a stream of low-value, low-fee work from clients, which is often currently completed by junior employees.

The software cannot, however, provide advice. It can identify, for example, the presence of particular clause types in a contract, or produce a particular type of contract. But it cannot advise of the actions that should be taken as a result of the presence of a clause type, or whether a generic contract type should be adapted given the specific circumstances of the client. As a result, the software is designed to enable clients to address basic issues quickly and cheaply. It does not replace the advisory role of an accountant or lawyer. Software can strengthen relationships between a firm and its clients. By providing software to a client, the firm has a means of consolidating a client relationship through the client's everyday use of the software provided and, most importantly, through the cross-referring of work to different practice groups when the issue at hand requires advice as well as basic analysis and document production. This link between the software and client relationship is further examined below in relation to the four paths firms can take to become a software provider.

Four paths

Firms that embark on the journey to become providers of software need to make a number of decisions:
(1) Whether to sell software to clients or (2) co-develop software with clients. Both paths have been followed. The first involves the law firm developing a viable software product before approaching multiple existing and potential clients and offering it as a product. The second involves working with existing clients to identify a stream of work currently completed by the accounting or law firm that software could assist with and allow the client to complete in-house. A collaborative proof of concept project then leads to the development of the

software, which may be bespoke for the client.
(3) Whether to charge using a subscription model or (4) charge as part of a preferred supplier model. The former involves the firm charging the client according to their usage of the software, whether by user license, data reviewed, contracts generated, etc. The latter involves providing the software to clients free of charge, on condition that all of their more complex work is offered to the law or accounting firm. Decisions about which path to follow are, in part at least, dependent on the nature of the relationship with the clients using the software. Established client relationships lend themselves more to the co-development and preferred supplier model; providing software helps deepen such relationships. New client relationships are more suited to the selling software and subscription models.

To code or not to code

Traditionally, accounting and law firms have not had the skills required for software development. As a result, one of the most common questions is whether firms should employ computer coders or programmers or work with existing software firms to develop their products. There is no consensus on the best approach, and both are used by firms in the UK. A key consideration is whether the firm can identify an external software firm to work with that has both the knowledge of the sector and ability to meet the firm's strict procurement rules. Another consideration is whether the firm wants to set up a separate group or entity to host its software activities, sometimes badged as 'software solutions' units, as this may provide an easier way to bring in coding or programming expertise.

What is clear, however, is that whether accounting and law firms begin to employ coders or programmers, or work with existing software firms, there is a need for the development of multi-disciplinary expertise. To be an accounting or law firm that is a software provider requires the embedding of accounting or legal technologists (those with knowledge of both accounting/law and technology) into the operations of the firm. These individuals ensure the link between the software and accounting or legal practice is effective, both in terms of how the software handles accounting or legal questions and how the software is used to build relationships with clients. Often this means employing technologists with experience of accounting or legal practice, perhaps as a paralegal or junior, but who have since retrained and now have knowledge of coding or programming. These individuals act as crucial bridges between lawyers who provide advice, and the software used by clients.

From accounting or law firm to professional service provider

The firm as software provider signals a change in the business model of the firm. Arguably, the switch is from accounting or law firm to accountancy or legal service provider. The former is focused on providing advice about accounting/the law and accounting/legal solutions to clients; the latter involves firms in both providing advice to clients on complex matters and enabling clients to address their own basic legal issues through a wider service offering that includes software. The switch to acting as a service provider with a wider offering to clients is, however, not just about developing new products such as software. It also involves reimagining what a firm looks like. The range of people employed within the firm is likely to change, exemplified by the importance of accounting and legal technologists. And the firm is likely to collaborate more widely with a range of suppliers and alliances, such as software development companies.

> "So, I don't necessarily see that the adoption of AI is going to erode law firms' business models. I think it will develop them and provide new opportunities for revenue as law firms start selling AI solutions to clients. But I don't see it as a threat to the kind of law firm business model."

3.4.2 Case 2: The accounting or law firm as data analyser

> " … our clients within our industry are becoming really hungry for insights that we can tell them from the data that we hold about them and predictions of what might happen next."

Extending the remit of the advisor

As a trusted and commercial advisor, the role of an accountant or lawyer has always extended beyond solving the specific legal problem presented by the client. The use of artificial intelligence in document review and case analysis provides an opportunity to develop new forms of data that can extend the advisor role in new directions. By generating data about the type of accounting and legal issues resolved for clients and patterns in their occurrence, cause, resolution and impacts, the accounting or legal advisor is able to use data as a new source of insight, and then offer clients new services that extend beyond matter-specific counsel. Advice can be provided about approaches to ongoing accounting and legal risk management and business planning informed by analysis of patterns in data. Examples include spotting patterns in the causes of, or resolutions to accounting poor practice or litigation that can be used to prevent or effectively resolve future issues; or predicting the likely costs of different legal resolutions to disputes to allow clients to better manage their liabilities.

Systematic analysis of professional work

To become a data analyser a firm has to adopt a more systematic approach to accounting or legal work. Before analysis can occur, data has to be generated. This means capturing information about accounting and legal activities in a systematised and standardised way. As a result, the following are needed:

- Clear workflows: Each case or project needs to proceed through the same stages, with defined information being recorded at each stage.
- Systematised data recording: The important pieces of information about a case or project need to be identified and ways of recording the information created, using standardised codes that allow future analysis of patterns.
- Analytical frameworks: For each matter type a series of parameters for analysis needs to be identified relating to

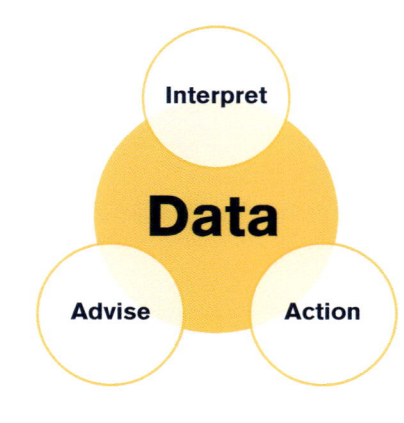

Figure 1. The triumvirate of the data analysing firm.

issues such as cause, resolution and client costs. Each of these will require a range of data fields to be recorded to allow effective analysis. As a result, analytical framework and data recording need to inform one another. Firms that are data analysers need, therefore, to rethink the way they project manage cases, both to ensure the establishment and following of workflows and to ensure the quality of the data generated.

Making use of data

What can accounting and law firms do with the data and analysis they generate? As Figure 1 shows, there is a triumvirate that underlies the data analysing firm.

Interpret: The firm needs not only to identify the patterns and trends in the data, but also to interpret them for the client. What do they reveal, why is the trend significant, and what questions does this pose for the client?

Advise: Once the data has been interpreted, the firm can advise the client on how they should respond to the insights generated. This most commonly takes the form of advice about accounting, legal or management strategies that can reduce risk and the occurrence of future problems, and the minimisation of costs associated with resolving such issues. Advice is, then, about practical steps for changing the patterns and trends that create problems or costs for the client.

Action: The firm can play an active role in implementing the advice provided to the client. This can involve a range of actions, from working with firm management, in-house accountants or counsel to develop new approaches or legal structures that reduce risk, to providing training to the client's employees which allows them to act in ways that avoid problems arising (e.g., in future audits or in employment disputes).

The triumvirate of interpret-advise-action thus provides a way that the firm as data analyser can exploit data for the client's benefit and provide a new kind of service offering that extends the idea of the trusted advisor.

Broadening the client offering

The data analysing firm can provide a broader client offering. An issue firms must resolve, however, is the extent to which they charge clients for the insights that data provide. Most firms are adopting a two-pronged approach to broadening the client offering:

- Data interpretation and advice is increasingly provided as one of the constituent parts of services. As clients seek to reduce their accounting and legal costs, law firms are responding by using data interpretation and advice both to help clients identify ways of reducing cost, and to demonstrate the value-add of using a firm's services. This is a trade-off, as firms potentially reduce demand for their work through advice designed to minimise clients' accounting problems or legal risk while at the same time demonstrating the value of using their services and thus securing long-term relationships and bolstering the ability of in-house accountants or counsel to defend spend on professional services.
- Firms generate additional revenue streams through the actions prompted by data interpretation and advice. Clients pay law firms to help implement actions that reduce risk or the cost of resolving accounting or legal matters.

"

You know what, we've got tons of data that we've captured for years and years... So, we're now starting to look at what that data really means, can we predict where claims are going to come from, what the outcomes are going to be, what the compensation values are going to be? And then, can we then go behind that to try and do a bit more preventative to reduce the numbers of claims and do some stuff with that?"

The data analysing firm is likely, then, to broaden its offering to clients as a means of offsetting pressures around fees and efficiency, with the range of lines of revenue generation being expanded.

3.4.3 Case 3: The accounting or law firm as process and project consultant

> "If you think about the upfront investment in creating an in-house counsel education content, we have to be able to probably do it once and sell it many times…"

Law and accounting firms are using technology for more than the improvement of their own process efficiency or the delivery of better legal and accounting services to their clients. They are also using technology to help their clients manage a wider set of their own organisational processes, and to support clients' change projects.

The need for process thinking

Accounting and law firms have not traditionally paid attention to their own or their clients' business processes. Accountants and lawyers are used to working in their own bespoke ways and, while a sequence of widely recognised stages exists in any piece of work, it is rare for the stages to be process mapped or for the work to be formally project managed to coordinate different stages and their interactions. The services of accountants and lawyers to their clients, whilst commercially informed and oriented, have also been disconnected from the fine-grained detail of the client's work processes and their ongoing management.

The accounting and law firm as process and project manager signals a change, because of the need for process engineering and management for the deployment of AI technologies. Both in terms of having the data required for AI technologies to operate, and in terms of understanding where and when in a piece of work AI can be deployed, work process mapping and management is important both within the accounting or law firm and within the client firm. By adopting a process management perspective, accounting and law firms are also able to provide the client with a new level of visibility around the services being provided. Once work processes are mapped and clear stages of work identified, it becomes possible to use project management software that not only facilitates work process management but also provides to clients, through a dashboard-style online system, details about the work the firm is doing for them at any particular time.

The opportunities that process management brings

For accounting and law firms, the challenge of work process mapping and management should not be underestimated. It is a significant break from the norms of how they operate. But the reasons for considering such a move are simple; it provides the best way to identify opportunities for using AI and allows a new service to client in the form of a dashboard charting progress on their case. Such dashboards can also be used to allow the client to communicate directly with the professionals working for them, and even provide the documentation and data needed.

For clients, engaging in their own work process mapping and engineering can not only help drive efficiencies, it can also ensure they can provide the kind of files and data needed by their law and accounting service providers. Of course, clients are not going to engage in mapping just to facilitate the work of their accountants and lawyers. However, it is increasingly common for clients to look to their professional advisors for wider input on the management of their business. When coupled with the way new technologies encourage process mapping and management, services to clients that were once regarded as the domain of business and management consultancies are increasingly an opportunity for accounting and law firms. Once they have engaged with their clients to help map business processes for the purpose of AI implementation, law and accounting firms are well placed to offer advice to clients on how to redesign and improve their business generally.

Once law and accounting firms have developed detailed insights into their clients' processes, and assembled structured data on them, they can offer project management services. These go beyond advising on process redesign and improvement, to encompass more significant, project-based internal change initiatives. In one example, a client struggled with the need to manage the training and development of its staff members, which had an impact on employment law-related matters handled by the law firm. The law firm was aware of a software product that could solve the client's problems and was able to advise about its implementation. This created opportunities to capture data from the system to support the client's operations, as well as potentially feed into the analysis of the client's employment law-related issues.

Enabling the move to a project manager approach
As accounting and law firms consider mapping and managing their own business processes, and advising their clients about their processes, it's clear that skills associated with case management, project management and management advice are increasingly important within the professional services firm. In this model, firms need to combine accounting or legal experts with professionals with different skillsets, both to map and project manage work within the accounting and law firm, and to advise clients on such issues. Often with a background in accounting or law, these individuals have the expertise to effectively map, (re)engineer and project manage in a way that complements the firm's accounting and legal expertise.

Indeed, when client advisory opportunities arise around work process management and the use of technology, some firms have opted for a dedicated team of professionals responsible for change management and process (re)engineering for clients using new technology. These teams are not populated exclusively by accountants or lawyers. Accounting and legal technologists, project managers and analysts are increasingly engaging in client interactions and service delivery as the accounting and law firm service offer expands.

> "I think technology will drive us to a compliance service being carried out quicker, more efficiently, and I think we'll end up being able to add far more value on the consultancy piece. So, I think staff just get redeployed into different areas of the work and I think the compliance piece will be devalued and the consultancy piece will be valued at a far higher figure."

3.4.4 Case 4: The accounting or law firm as automated business

> "The other observation I'd make about where AI is starting to be used is in looking at unstructured data, the analysis of unstructured data predominantly for internal purposes of improving internal efficiency."

The ability of AI to continuously learn and use predictive algorithms has been most successfully applied to routine, simple and laborious tasks. Despite these often rather circumscribed domains of application, such uses in the practice of legal and accounting services tend, in the mainstream discussion, to overshadow the use of AI in support of managing the business of professional services. Automating aspects of the business of accounting or law – functions associated with running the firm – has the potential to allow mid-tier firms to remain competitive. Practice management software is becoming less alien to professional services firms, and AI creates a new opportunity to look at specific tasks associated with the way accounting and law firms operate, and to reduce time spent on them, both by professionals and support staff.

How can AI help?

AI's primary contribution to the business of law or accounting is to save time with unavoidable, repetitive tasks. Using AI's ability to recognise patterns and recurrent processes can allow the creation and interrogation of data that is currently completed manually. Two examples illustrate this potential. A number of AI-based products now offer 'smart' time recording. When integrated with email systems and other software used to communicate with clients, these systems can identify how long has been spent drafting and sending communications to clients and then automatically record this information in time records and billing systems. Some firms are buying products available in the market, while others have developed their own.

Another common use of AI is to manage data subject access requests. These requests are made both by employees – often when they leave the firm – and by clients. Under GDPR regulations firms must respond to such requests, but this can involve accessing and searching a large corpus of data, including emails and other official documents. Firms cannot bill clients for these requests and therefore need efficient ways of responding. AI can provide an efficient and cost-effective way of scanning the corpus of data to identify potentially relevant materials. In some ways, this is similar to the use of AI for e-disclosure and other forms of document review. The difference is that AI is not used to identify particular contractual forms or patterns of transactions, as part of the practice of law or accounting, but to identify documents relevant to a particular subject access request, as part of the business of running a professional services firm. In addition, as discussed in the case of 'firms as process and project managers', a move towards a process management logic and the (re)engineering of processes also encourages the use of technology to manage the business of accounting and law.

The nascent application of AI to the business of law and business of accounting

Less attention has been given to how AI can help with managing the business of accounting and law. But there is growing interest, and firms are increasingly analysing their professional work and administrative processes for opportunities to use AI. From a client perspective, the advantage of adopting AI in the business of accounting and law is the reduced overhead costs that, ultimately, must be passed on to clients. From the firm's perspective, as well as reducing overheads, AI can take on some of the more mundane and time-consuming aspects of work, time-billing being a particularly good example. This makes the use of AI attractive to professionals and means the use of AI to address issues associated with the business of accounting and law can be a good first step to exposing professionals to the benefits technology can bring.

> "In the traditional audit practice what we've been trying to do for the last two, three years is use tech as much as we can… either to be more efficient, so that we can get more done, or to be more intelligent. So, rather than somebody sitting there and putting stuff up manually, it's using tech to do that, or helping us to get to data far more quickly so we can sit with a client and advise them rather than spending ages churning numbers out."

Image: Sora Shimazaki on Pexels

3.4.5 Case 5: The efficient law or accounting firm

> "But it's basically admin, it's not being a lawyer."

Greater client demands
Clients increasingly require cost reduction and predictability combined with expectations of a fixed price for a particular piece of work, rather than a billable hours' basis. Hence, there is an incentive for law firms to become more efficient. The efficient law firm uses software capabilities and associated work redesign to significantly reduce the time and cost of carrying out repetitive, high-volume tasks such as document review. This means that the firm can complete these stages in a particular matter in a shorter time, with fewer person-hours and, hence, lower staff costs.

The basic idea
Software applications can use machine learning to search for particular concepts, clauses or phrases in large numbers of documents such as commercial or employment contracts or emails, or patterns of data entry in accounting systems. This is work that would previously have been done manually by junior staff working long hours, often under great time pressure. The main outcome of the process is that anomalous clauses or other details requiring lawyers' or accountants' attention can quickly and consistently be identified. Other benefits include being able to provide structure to poorly organised document sets, making ongoing document management and revision more efficient and effective. And, if the AI is trained correctly, the human error that results from working under pressure on very repetitive tasks can be eliminated.

Choosing suitable applications
Implementing and training the software requires up-front effort. And the data or documents to be reviewed need to be in sufficiently large quantities, and of sufficiently consistent structure, for the training process to work. This means that the efficient law firm is selective in its use of software for document review and similar tasks. The application needs to be one where the effort involved in training the software will be justified by the cost and time savings, and by the improvements in accuracy that may result.

Using software is not a free lunch. There is typically a variable cost associated with using software for tasks such as document review, on a per document basis. Training of the AI is still required on a job-by-job basis to reflect the idiosyncrasies of a particular client or project, especially at this stage in the development of the software and of firms' maturity in using it. And this training often needs to be done by staff experienced in the substantive legal or accounting content of the work, so that the right judgment calls can be made about such issues as the equivalences in meaning between slightly different terms across a disparate set of documents. One firm found that using too diverse or inexperienced a team of people to train the AI led to a very inconsistent and inaccurate outcome.

As well as the basic parameters of scale and structure of documents and data, it is important to consider, especially at this stage in adoption maturity, the particular team and people involved. AI-enabled software needs to be deployed in propitious circumstances in terms of the aptitude and attitude of the team working on a particular client project, and the saliency and likelihood of success. Clearly, reducing a team's burden of repetitive work or increasing their client revenue is the best way to encourage and propagate wider adoption by well-informed users.

Directing effort and maximising impact

Using AI to extract documents and clauses for review means that, especially under time pressure, lawyers can direct their attention to the clauses that really matter rather than being forced to read whole documents, sometimes less thoroughly than they would like. In the accounting context, audit can be conducted in a more comprehensive way, and auditors' hunches and suspicions about anomalous entries followed up and explored more easily. And, where clauses recur in multiple documents, the effort expended in either confirming or modifying a clause in one document leads to an improvement that is scaled up over all the documents in which it occurs. In other words, there are efficiency gains in both diagnosis and remedy. Done well, such uses of AI-enabled technology can lead to a very clear-cut competitive advantage - i.e., winning business that would otherwise be out of reach. For example, where time pressure is an important factor – such as may arise in a merger, or when a deadline for a regulatory change requires clients to act quickly in relation to a large number of contracts or business units – the speed of AI-enabled software can lead the efficient law or accounting firm to bid with confidence for challenging tasks.

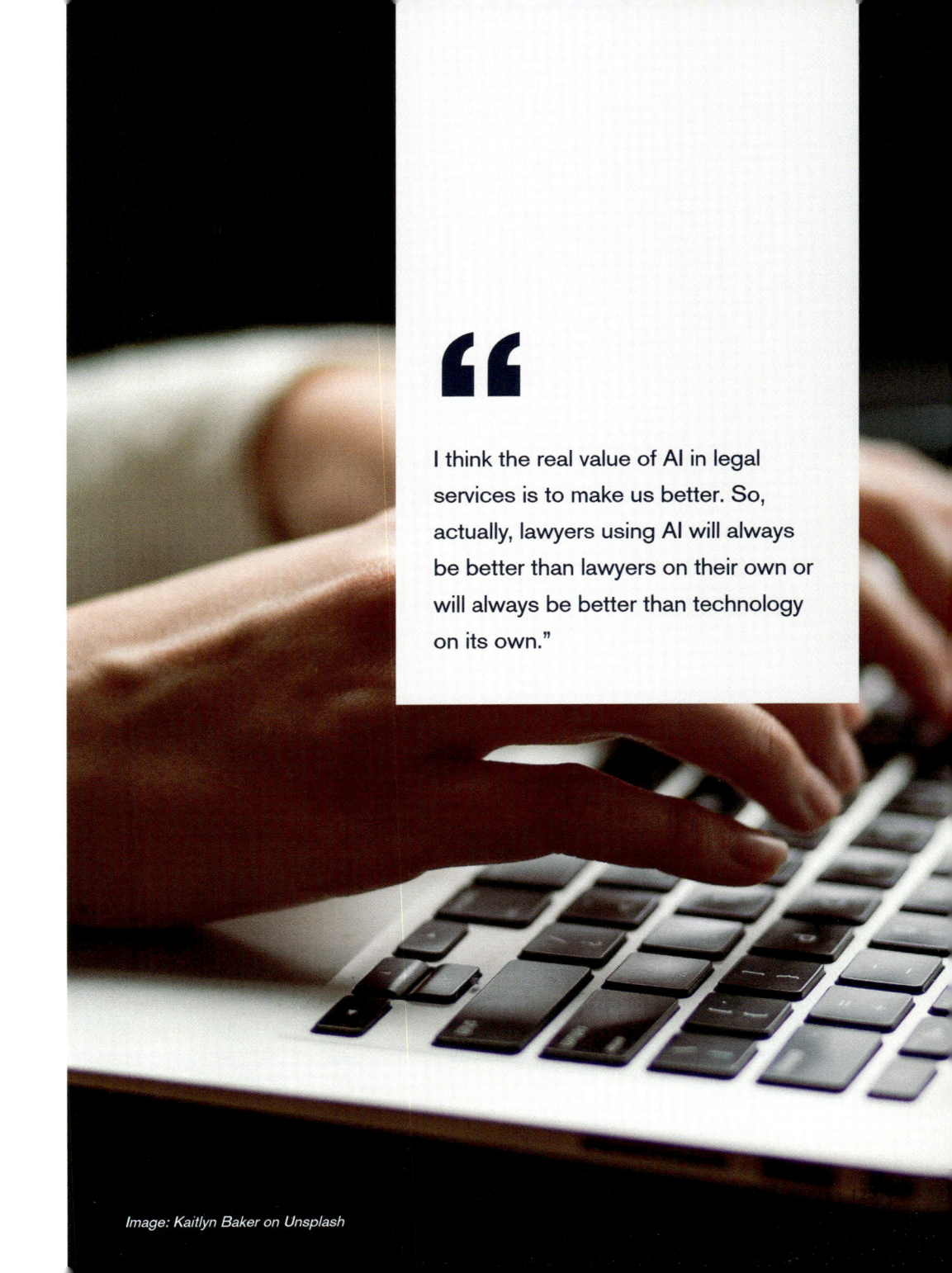

> "I think the real value of AI in legal services is to make us better. So, actually, lawyers using AI will always be better than lawyers on their own or will always be better than technology on its own."

Image: Kaitlyn Baker on Unsplash

3.4.6 Case 6: The (re)integrated law or accounting firm – capturing value

> "…sometimes you would just get part of the deal and the due diligence would be done by a smaller law firm or something. But now that we have that AI tool, they say, 'why don't you just do everything?"

The division of labour
As in any industry, firms in the legal and accounting sectors specialise. They specialise in different areas of practice, types of client, and stages in the processes used to deliver their services. Process specialisation sees tasks divided up between firms according to the capabilities required and the cost of delivering them. Labour-intensive work, such as document review, may be outsourced to firms with lower overheads and wage rates, in some cases by offshoring to countries with much lower labour costs. While this generates inevitable additional challenges in defining, contracting for, and controlling the delivery of outsourced tasks, the cost savings are seen to justify the practice.

Technology changes the economics of outsourcing
The use of software to radically reduce the labour content of tasks such as document review means that the cost advantage of outsourcing to lower-cost firms and locations is reduced or disappears altogether. The integrated – or re-integrated – law or accounting firm can then complete the whole process in-house and retain direct control over service delivery, removing the risk associated with contracting with a third party. They also eliminate the need to pay for the outsourced work and so, assuming that the AI-enabled technology can efficiently be used to carry out the more repetitive tasks, the re-integrated firm can also capture all the value of the work themselves.

Pressure from clients and courts
Tendering processes – especially for larger and more sophisticated clients – increasingly include a focus on the use of AI-enabled technology. Professional service providers are required to explain how they intend to use technology in executing a project. In the legal context, courts are applying pressure to law firms to use technology as a way to reduce court costs. These various pressures also militate toward the law or accounting firm adopting AI-enabled technology to carry out routine and repetitive tasks in-house rather than outsourcing them, which might mean they risk failing to satisfy the requirements of would-be clients' purchasing criteria and needing to justify their decisions and attendant costs to courts and other authorities.

Building capability
As well as satisfying requirements of clients and external authorities, bringing activity in-house also contributes to the development of firms' capabilities in the use of AI-enabled technology. Re-integrating firms are developing in-house technical consultancy units and technology-capable legal and accounting staff so that, in responding to external requirements and in developing their strategy in a more pro-active way, they are less dependent on technology consultants from providers of expertise in out-sourced solution providers.

Image: Jason Leung on Unsplash

> "Clients have already reached a point where they might not be giving us that work or they're really reluctant to give us that work. So, the interest point is shifting that right onto the client's lap and saying, 'do you want to self-serve?' and then we put a service wrapper around that… again, that's allowed us to commoditise a service to a really high degree."

3.4.7 Case 7: The accounting or law firm as innovation lab

> "…the lab is set up for us to work with early-stage technology companies, primarily on product market fit, really helping them understand what the problem is, helping them create a product that is fit to take on that problem; and we will hopefully continue to work with those companies once they become lab portfolio companies."

Emerging technologies and their increasing speed and power have created opportunities in accounting and law, but also created a dilemma; what should be the relationship between accounting and law firms and technology providers? Should professional services firms become tech firms, developing their own AI technologies? Should they look for 'off the shelf' products? Or should they enter into a collaboration with a tech start-up? These questions arise because the development of new technologies and the way they shape accounting and legal services requires dialogue between those able to develop the technology and the professionals who will use it. Therefore, we see accounting and law firms experimenting with a range of approaches.

The in-house approach

Some firms are using in-house development, although this is still relatively rare because of the scale of resource needed. Those firms that have employed coders and technology experts tend to use them for relatively small in-house projects (e.g., providing chat bots to allow professionals to search the firm's business support services such as HR) and/or to provide a bridge to a technology start-up they may be collaborating with. Such firms often categorise themselves as 'tech savvy'. They encourage professionals to engage in coding – for example, by providing basic training for anyone interested – and professionals often get involved in developing or customising products, in addition to their daily work. In this setup, accountants and lawyers work alongside the in-house coders and become 'hackers' focused on addressing challenges and opportunities which the technology is believed to provide. It is important for such initiatives to have firm-level sponsorship, and we have seen examples where partners become expert in coding languages such as Python and conduct workshops for other professionals. An in-house approach is often supported with a system to capture innovative ideas from employees within the firm. These systems invite suggestions from staff and create a forum to discuss, scrutinise and sometimes transform an idea into a technology project. In such initiatives, technological advancements come not only from tech start-ups or technology providers but also from within the firms. The challenge for such firms is to ensure that ideas are appropriately scrutinised internally, feedback is provided as appropriate, and only the most feasible and value-adding projects taken forward.

The proof-of-concept approach

Some firms are developing proof-of-concept (POC) projects in which technologies are co-developed with start-up providers. This is most common when the accounting or law firm has spotted a specific opportunity and identified a start-up that can provide a solution. In such cases, the accounting or law firm needs to provide staff time to develop the new technology, given that professionals work with the start-up company to make the solution appropriate and viable, and money to part-fund its development, with agreement about future licensing arrangements. The POC approach can also stimulate new collaboration between professionals, as technology-competent lawyers or accountants from different areas of the business come together with technology providers to work on the POC project. It may also stimulate greater involvement with clients interested in the new product. POC projects can engage professionals in a conversation about the potential of technology, raise awareness of the opportunities it creates, and at the same time dispel the myth of AI being there to replace professionals, which can proliferate when professionals are not involved in the specification and development of technology.

The incubator approach

Some firms provide space for new start-ups to incubate their ideas within the firm. This allows the firm to not only stay up to date with the rapid evolution of AI, but also to steer the direction of product development in line with their needs. By providing an 'incubator' space firms avoid the need for initial financial investment beyond the time and space needed to support the incubator but can still get the first option on a technology before it is offered to others in the market. Incubators provide start-ups with mentorship and a defined number of hours of 'advice' from accountants and lawyers about how to make a technology attractive and viable. Sometimes the accounting or law firm will offer investment to take the start-up's vision from concept to reality, but this often only occurs later in the process when feasibility and benefits are clear. Start-ups not only have access to accountants and lawyers to test and polish their ideas, but also to clients. This also arguably provides benefits to clients, as they get visibility of how technology might enhance their professional advisors' offer. Indeed, accounting and law firms see incubators as an opportunity not only to test the future direction of technologies but also the changing needs and demands of clients. Those providing space to start-ups to incubate their ideas sense that, by being at the forefront of technological advancement, they can increase their market share by becoming a source of future technological innovation that attracts clients. The final step in an incubator process involves the accounting or law firm not only adopting the technology, but also taking a stake in the start-up if its product gains market traction. But this end point does not have to be the priority. The benefit of an incubator is the capacity and opportunity to better understand and shape new technology and widen awareness within the accounting or law firm. There is also a marketing element to this exercise, where host firms enhance their reputation in the eyes of clients.

3.5 Approaches to the deployment of AI in accounting and law firms in England

This section provides a summary of insights from research into approaches taken when deploying AI in accounting and law firms in England. The approaches are anonymous examples of how the firms studied have gone about developing their AI readiness. Six exemplary approaches are presented, each dealing with one or more of the challenges of deploying AI in accounting and law firms. Firms often use more than one of the approaches documented, but this section is not intended to be a list of approaches that must be followed. Instead, it is a stimulus for firms as they consider ways of responding to the challenges of becoming AI ready. As such, firms might choose the approach(es) most closely related to the challenge(s) they face.

Image: Fauxels on Pexels

3.5.1 Approach 1: Addressing the AI competency challenge

> "We certainly have people working in our teams now who are technology specialists first and accountants second."
>
> "20% of the people that are coming into the business need to be data scientists… We haven't got to that point yet. I don't think we're very far away from it."

One of the most common challenges faced by accounting and law firms is to understand what AI can (and cannot) do, and how to deploy it successfully within the firm. It is tempting to assume that the market can help firms solve this problem – i.e., to assume that there is a way to identify a supplier who will provide the technology and help deploy it within the firm. However, whilst there are undoubtedly many firms offering AI solutions, selecting the right supplier and effectively embedding the technology in the firm requires more than a successful procurement process. Firms must ask themselves: do we have the people within the firm, with the right competency, to help us to deploy AI effectively? By using 'we' this question implies that firms need to employ people with some degree of AI competency. This does not necessarily mean coding abilities. It can mean someone able to evaluate technologies and their appropriateness for the firm, understand how to implement them, and assist with their use on a day-to-day basis. How to address this challenge?

Encourage the hobbyist

Many firms have tech-savvy professionals who are keen experimenters. These individuals, out of personal interest, have often kept up to speed with the latest developments in AI technology. They are also knowledgeable about the firm's business and the ways AI may be appropriate and fit with existing strategy. If a firm has one or more hobbyist, one option is to empower the individual(s) to lead the firm's assessment and deployment of AI. By giving them the time and resource to properly assess possibilities, and design implementation projects for new technologies, a firm can benefit from a blend of AI knowledge and firm familiarity. The individual can become a leader in the assessment of which opportunities to pursue, which suppliers to use, and in the implementation and day-to-day use of the technology.

Bring in an accounting/law technologist

If the firm does not have a hobbyist or cannot release them, the alternative is to recruit a technologist who can bring expertise into the firm to assess opportunities and manage implementation. Usually, a technologist will have experience in accounting or law, as abstract understanding of the use of AI/technology from other contexts is often hard to translate and can lead to a lack of appreciation of the ways of working in accounting or law and requirements of regulators and clients.

The main challenge with this approach is the scarcity of technologists: individuals with both technical knowledge and accounting/law experience are in short supply and hard to recruit. The main message is that firms need to develop in-house AI competency. This is a crucial step in the process of becoming ready and able to assess the opportunities and implement strategies. It is also crucial to remember that the accounting/law technologist is not a back-office para-professional, nor should their function be seen as IT-department related. The technologist is someone able to marry technology and accounting/law expertise. They will become central to the activities of the firm, including in front of clients when pitching, hence the fundamental importance to AI readiness of identifying the right person with the right competency.

3.5.2 Approach 2: The adoption dilemma

> "You can imagine you've got your head office that's basically saying to you 'right you've now got to implement this, then this, then this'. Then we changed tax software. Then we added on AI. Now we're taking away the existing software for accounts jobs. I think they're just a little bit like, 'back off! We've had enough'."

One of the most common dilemmas faced by accounting and law firms is how to ensure the adoption across the firm of any new technologies. Professional services firms are all too familiar with resistance, from partners in particular, to changes in ways of working. This can prevent new initiatives from succeeding. The Next Generation Professional Services Firm project has identified multiple insights into what can both prevent and enable the adoption of new technologies. The key decision that firms need to take about their approach is whether to impose new technologies and ways of working or diffuse them gradually across the firm.

Imposition

One approach, after a period of trialling a new technology/approach, is to impose its use across the firm. The advantage of doing this is the potential for a speedier roll-out and greater consistency across the firm, both of which are beneficial in terms of client service offering. The disadvantage is the potential for significant resistance from partners and others, which in the worst-case scenario can result either in partners exiting the firm or post-hoc compromises that undermine adoption as exceptions or compromises are negotiated. If an imposition approach is taken, the firm must ensure:

- The technology is tried and tested, delivers what it promises, and is adequately supported during the transition, including in terms of accounting/legal technologists to work with professionals and help them get what they need from the system. Do not impose a system that has glitches, is difficult to use and does not always deliver effectively what is required by professionals. Stress test the system first.
- The message is clear about what the technology will deliver; expectations need to be managed (see below). Over-promising leads to disappointment, annoyance and an easy line of resistance. Be clear about what the technology can and cannot do, what will be gained, what will be difficult, what will stay the same and why the pain of change is worthwhile in tangible terms for professionals themselves and for clients.
- Time is taken to generate some consensus. If a majority supports imposition of the technology, even reluctantly, the minority are more likely to be swayed. Professionals are most likely to be influenced by their peers, so ensure you have a large enough group of supporters who can help convince the sceptics, or at least make them nervous that they might be resisting something that ultimately proves beneficial.

> "We've got a champion in each office… they are comfortable with that."

Diffusion

An alternative is gradual diffusion of a technology throughout the firm from a niche in one or more teams or practice groups. The advantage of diffusion is that it helps avoid some of the most destructive forms of resistance and allows technologies to be deployed where and when appropriate. The disadvantage is that diffusion can be slow, inconsistent, and lead to parallel ways of working. A diffusion approach relies on some mechanism of comparison between teams, practice groups or offices so that non-adopters are aware of what adopters are doing, what benefits they might be gaining, and how the technology has changed their work. If using a diffusion approach, things to consider include:

- Allowing everyone access to the technology from the start. It is likely to be counter-productive if teams or practice groups are 'chosen', as others might feel excluded and thus less willing to learn from the early adopters. There will then be a natural opt-in process by the most enthusiastic, with those less certain waiting and watching.
- Ensuring awareness of what those adopting the technology are doing and achieving. Professionals are well-known for being interested in what their peers are doing, and keen not to fall behind. Diffusion will occur naturally if the achievements of early adopters are visible; others will not want to be left behind. Examples of how clients respond to what the early adopters are doing are particularly powerful. No professional likes to think that their peers are better able to provide outstanding service to clients.
- Leveraging professional relationships and respect. Diffusion occurs best when individuals learn from those they respect. Ensure that early adopters who are well known and respected by other professionals in the firm act as vectors for diffusion. This must happen organically. Respect is not created by the ceremonial conferment of the role of 'exemplar' onto an individual, respect is earned. The most effective way of driving diffusion is to allow individuals to interact with, build relationships with and gain the respect of their peers in a low pressure, organic way without forcing diffusion by tasking an individual with convincing others. This will take time.

Whether imposition or diffusion is chosen, it is important to remember that the process of adopting a new technology requires careful planning and management, over months and years. A balance must be struck between the urgency of change and its impact on the culture of the firm. It should also be recognised that there can be transition points as the strategy develops. For example, a diffusion approach could switch to imposition once the majority of teams or practice groups has adopted a new technology.

> "I don't see the AI taking over the expert's role. I would probably imagine that the focus of the expert might change so they might not be performing as much of the testing they once were, but the analysis of the results and the conclusion still needs to lie with the expert… I think it will just free up the experts to do some different work rather than it taking over their role."

3.5.3 Approach 3: Managing expectations

For many professionals, the possibilities of AI are unfamiliar and hard to reconcile with their understanding of accounting or legal practice. Firms face a challenge in helping professionals develop realistic expectations about what AI can do. Expectations are often either too high, and even hyperbolic, or too low, because of a failure to understand what AI can deliver. An important approach to becoming AI-ready, therefore, is to work with professionals to help them understand what AI means for their practice. When managing the expectations of professionals some important things to consider are:

The need to address the 'jobs' discourse directly

The idea of AI 'stealing' jobs is all too common. In professional services firms the current state of AI is predominantly about practice enhancements allowing professionals to do things for clients they couldn't do before. Being clear about the purpose of AI readiness – which is rarely intended to replace people with computers and usually involves providing more sophisticated services – is an important starting point for discussions.

The potential for misunderstanding what AI can do

To date there are few if any AI applications that replace what human professionals do. Some allow part of a task to be speeded up; for example, e-discovery and document review. However, this still leaves human professionals with the most complicated elements of interpreting the significance of the output of AI. Other AI applications allow a completely different form of analysis and advice to clients, thus transforming the service offering through new approaches that often complement rather than replace existing approaches. Being clear about what AI can do, why it is useful, and what this means for professional practice is thus crucial so professionals understand what to expect and do not have too high or too low expectations for how AI will change their work.

The limited scope of AI impacts

For many professionals, AI will be one input into their practice, and they may not even use the AI applications themselves, instead needing to know how to use the outputs of applications in their work. It is important, therefore, to be clear and realistic about who will need to become 'AI savvy'. In other words, knowing who will need to use applications directly, who will need to know how to read the analyses generated by AI, and who might not be affected at all.

Use data to manage expectations

Professionals respond well to evidence, so collect and present evidence of what AI can do (for example, through pilots). Present the data in a way that accepts the limitations, does not over-claim in terms of efficiencies, innovativeness or value added, but clearly shows what is gained.

Help recalibrate professionals' understandings of excellence

One of the most fundamental challenges is to recalibrate how professionals understand excellent practice, given the affordances of AI. In many cases new technology allows professionals to conduct analysis, and provide advice to clients, that would not have been possible in the past (for instance, 100% samples in auditing, or risk reviews and pattern detection across thousands of contracts). Similarly, the data available to inform decisions is often different. As a result, firms need to help professionals understand how AI will not simply reproduce their current ways of working but introduce new approaches, with definitions of excellent practice and advice in turn being redefined and extended into new domains. This is important because without such recalibration professionals are likely to assess AI using an existing understanding of excellence. This often leads to disappointment and disillusionment, as new technology in many cases does not allow existing approaches to be carried out more quickly or accurately, leading professionals to see few benefits. Professionals thus need to learn about new possibilities so as to evaluate and appreciate AI in terms of the new opportunities and methods it enables.

Firms must, then, help professionals understand and appreciate AI, by managing their expectations and the frames of evaluation used when assessing a technology. This is a specific piece of work in itself and must be done sensitively. Again, as in the discussion of diffusion above, this learning often occurs best when it involves one professional learning from another they respect.

3.5.4 Approach 4: Who needs to use AI in the next generation professional services firm?

> "We are seeing the rise of these new roles such as a legal technologist, people who know about law, but they are mainly the people who are using technology. So, going forward, do we see that if we have enough work, we can have a dedicated team whose only job is to use AI, putting the documents in and then there's the output given to the lawyers?"

Whether AI is being used to automate tasks and processes or develop new client offerings through data analysis, an important question is, who needs the expertise to use the AI systems? Firms have responded to this question in two ways; by establishing a helpdesk, with a core group of expert users called on by everyone else to answer queries and use AI to deliver specified outcomes; or via a firm-wide roll-out that supports the use of AI systems across all teams, with champions helping with training and initial adoption.

Helpdesk delivered solutions

The helpdesk approach allows firms to organise the use of AI technologies (often using email or dedicated ticketing-systems) through a small team of experts. These experts use AI driven systems to perform a requested job and deliver the outputs to the teams handling a particular matter. In some instances, this helpdesk is not only aimed at internal requests, but also helps clients by allowing them either to use AI driven solutions provided by the firm, or to analyse the data generated by the professional services firm about their operations.

Over time, the helpdesk itself can become an expert system with automated proficiencies (e.g., managing a database of frequently raised queries or issues and their best solutions). This process may lead to the helpdesk becoming more systematically organised as there is a move from resolving requests in an ad-hoc manner to a repeatable and standardised manner. Most firms already have a version of a helpdesk – the IT department – but firms implementing AI need a separate AI-related helpdesk both because of the specific expertise required and because of the importance of viewing the use of AI as part of the client service offering, not as a back-office function (see above on the AI competency challenge).

The advantage of the helpdesk approach is the containment of the reskilling and adaptation process. Only a core team need to become expert in using AI systems, and this team can be staffed with enthusiasts committed to leveraging the systems. This means other professionals need not change many of their day-to-day practices, so long as they understand when AI-driven systems can assist and know they can call on the helpdesk for input. Firms might, however, find it difficult to sustain a helpdesk if the nature and volume of work cannot sustain a permanent core group. Another risk associated with the helpdesk approach is professionals ignoring the potential of AI, not calling the helpdesk and carrying on with traditional approaches. This can inhibit the full leverage of AI systems and lead to incomplete implementation. Helpdesks must, therefore, be backed up by an implementation plan that ensures teams make use of the helpdesk and incorporate AI-driven solutions into their practices.

Firm wide roll-out

This involves embedding the use of AI systems into the practices of teams, with all professionals working on matters where AI can help having the skills to use the systems. This means a wide group of professionals will complete training and know how to use the AI systems and interpret their outputs. An important step in firm wide roll-out is, therefore, identifying the professionals in each team who will use the

AI systems and ensuring they are trained. The most common approach to firm-wide roll-out is to deploy AI experts and enthusiasts as champions. Champions are system experts. They train others in the firm who are either interested in new technology or whose jobs have changed due to new technology. Training plays a vital role in ensuring individuals can use the technology effectively and preventing frustration, which can quickly creep in and lead to failed roll-out. Left to their own devices, busy law and accounting professionals who are potentially not enthusiastic about new technology will quickly find excuses for not using it.

The role of champions becomes even more central in instances where firms have adopted a top-down approach to rolling out new technology and making its usage mandatory (see above on the adoption dilemma). They can offer demonstrations of how new technology aids professionals with their work, and provide a swift response when problems are encountered. Champions also do more than just resolve technical issues. They are responsible for communicating with professionals about how technology will make their work better and benefit them. Filling the gap between expectations and hype and ensuring realistic expectations is crucial (see above on managing expectations). Champions are usually lawyers or accountants who are technology enthusiasts and understand the profession. They are therefore well placed to bridge the gap between technology use and professionals' needs. As noted elsewhere, they should be individuals respected across the firm since professionals learn best from others who they respect.

It is also important to remember that no innovation succeeds only because of enthusiasm. It also requires an adequate supporting infrastructure. It is the role of the champion to ensure that this infrastructure exists – hence they will need senior management support to ensure resource is in place to develop the infrastructure. The advantage of firm-wide roll-out is the widespread awareness and experience of AI systems it creates. It is also more adaptable to variable levels of work and demand for systems use than a helpdesk approach, given that those with the skills to use AI systems will also be qualified accountants/lawyers able to complete other tasks when AI inputs are not needed. The main disadvantage relates to the time and resources needed to ensure the skills exist across teams. Developing a group of champions and giving them the time to work with all teams is the crucial first step to overcoming this challenge.

3.5.5 Approach 5: Managing the change to the professional career path

> "I personally think the way the industry's going this whole accountancy partnership model will have to change, because at the moment it's very much based on audit partners and tax partners having a portfolio of clients that bring in a level of fees. And then you sort of get to a point where you've got enough experience and you can bring in enough money that you make partner. Well, that's not going to work anymore."

Another important challenge facing law and accounting firms that adopt AI-driven technologies is to develop appropriate career pathways for existing and newly recruited professionals. These pathways will exist alongside traditional pathways but must not be seen as second-rate routes given how important professionals on these pathways are, and will be, for the future of the firm. The new pathways will require both monetary and status rewards, such as partnership, that are equivalent to those on offer in traditional pathways.

New pathways are crucial for professionals who develop technological expertise that supports the development of innovative products and service offerings, but do not focus full-time on fee-earning work. These professionals will have accounting or legal expertise, and as such should be seen as having client-facing and not back office roles (see above on the AI competency challenge). However, they will not necessarily be key client relationship creators. Instead, they will provide crucial input into the production and delivery of services to clients won by other professionals. They will be the individuals working on AI helpdesks or embedded within teams and using AI to meet client needs (see above on who needs AI expertise). Crucially, those developing tech-based solutions for clients and finding opportunities for new technologies need to be recognised as generating revenues through the openings they create for others engaging directly with clients. As such, these individuals are fee earners, albeit indirectly, as their contributions allow others to more effectively attract and retain clients.

Until recently, professionals with technological expertise and not focusing full-time on fee earning would usually operate outside the partnership track. However, as technology becomes an integral part of modern law and accounting firms the new roles that support the use of AI-driven systems need to be incorporated within partnership paths, given that their contribution now and in the future will be equivalent to that of the traditional professional. Indeed, in many cases these individuals will be qualified accountants or lawyers who now use technology to support client services, and thus incorporating them into partnerships is not such a radical shift. It is, though, a crucial shift to ensure they feel they have a viable career route and can develop within the firm. Regulatory issues need to be navigated in some cases when individuals do not hold accounting or legal registrations. When this is the case, it may be necessary to offer para-partnership positions, such as Counsel or Principal. However, this approach should only be used when required by regulations, to ensure parity in reward and status for the new generation of professional technologists.

"Typically, partners would be at the top, probably going down towards, if you're looking in hierarchical terms, paralegals at the bottom of the tree. Ten years ago, no one batted an eyelid at that, but things are moving towards being much flatter structures."

> "Data importation is the big bottleneck because, as you say, if the data isn't standard somebody has to spend a lot of time mapping the data through, and that is highly inefficient. If somebody can solve that problem, I think it will go much, much quicker."

3.5.6 Approach 6: Organising digital and data driven professional services

> "Data interpretation is only as good as the data that's actually in the system, so you have to have a robust process of getting source documentation into the system. Rubbish in, rubbish out, as they say."

The adoption of AI involves two significant shifts for professional services firms; the move to more digital ways of working as technologies are incorporated into everyday practices, and the need to more effectively collect and organise the data needed by AI systems. Both of these shifts require different approaches to organising professional service work.

The use of digital technologies means **mapping and reengineering internal business processes** to allow AI technologies to be incorporated into accounting or law practice. This means dedicating individuals – who may be part of an innovation team, or one of the champions discussed above in relation to who needs to use AI – to the task of mapping how work is currently done, identifying opportunities to deploy AI and reengineering ways of working when needed. Although the initial stages of mapping and reengineering can be resource intensive, in the long term this work pays off thanks to the efficiencies or new client offerings that are made possible and leveraged again and again once the AI systems are in place.

In many ways, mapping and reengineering is like conducting a 'fly on the wall' analysis of the firm. The way things are currently done needs to be observed and recorded, the opportunities for AI identified, questions asked about changes needed to make the AI deployable, and then the need for reengineering identified. The final stage is to convince professionals to change in line with the reengineering plan (on this, see the points above regarding imposition, diffusion, creating AI champions, and so on).

The use of AI is also premised on collecting and analysing data. All AI systems need a database to work from, which must be curated by the firm. A crucial approach, early in any effort to deploy AI, is thus to review existing means of storing data, identify limitations, specify the data collection needed for the AI systems being planned, and ensure both that the infrastructure is in place to collect and store the data and that professionals understand how data needs to be collected and managed. This often involves bringing together multiple separate databases within the firm and putting data into a format and structure that is usable by AI systems.

A firm-wide strategy for collecting, analysing and sharing data across practice areas is thus crucial. This has technical elements relating to the database architecture, servers, and so on, as well as a crucial people element in that the data is only as good as the processes used by those collecting it, which in professionals service firms is the accountants and lawyers working for clients. It is, therefore, crucial that everyone collecting data and entering it into spreadsheets and systems understands how to format, name and systematise the data. Otherwise, the AI systems will not be able to use the data and thus will not function. The digital and data driven professional services firm is, then, an organisation that has particular ways of working and means of acquiring and storing data that are different to those in the professional services firm of the past. Taking seriously the need to change business and data processes is an essential part of the process of becoming AI ready.

Image: Negative Space Pexels

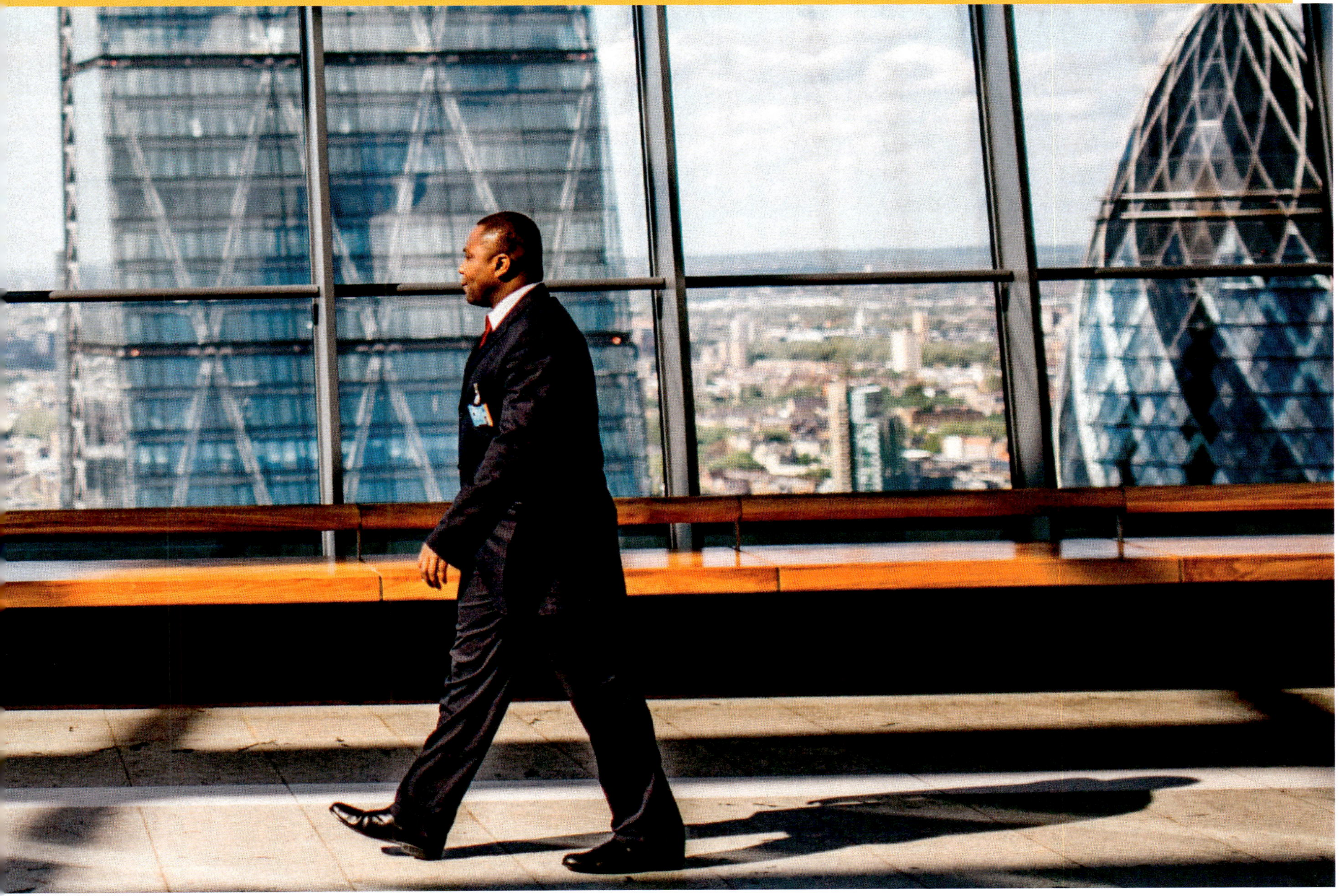

4 Exploring futures for professional services firms

4. Exploring futures for professional service firms

4.1	**Introducing scenarios and scenario planning**	**146**
	4.1.1 Why use scenarios?	**147**
	4.1.2 How we developed these scenarios	**148**
4.2	**Overview of the 2030 scenarios**	**150**
	4.2.1 Using scenarios to convert insights into action	**150**
	4.2.2 Using scenarios to help with organisational learning	**152**
	4.2.3 Building an anticipatory capacity in the firm	**152**
4.3	**Three scenarios for 2030**	**154**
	4.3.1 Scenario comparison table	**156**
4.4	**Scenario 1: Platform domination**	**158**
4.5	**Scenario 2: Bumpy superhighway**	**162**
4.6	**Scenario 3: Value kaleidoscope**	**168**
	Afterword	**175**

4.1 Introducing scenarios and scenario planning

The future is fundamentally uncertain, and the best leaders are those who accept this reality and find sensible ways to work with it. The three 2030 scenarios shared in this section are designed to help leaders in mid-size law and accounting firms acknowledge and work through future uncertainties so they can take decisions in the present. The novel COVID-19 pandemic that emerged in early 2020 highlighted the need for organisations of all kinds to ensure that their strategy remains robust and coherent under stress. It serves as the perfect example of a crisis that few anticipated, and fewer still prepared for. Taking the recent shared experience of COVID-19 as a starting point, this section invites you to take stock, assess what the future might look like and examine assumptions you make about the future. Such assumptions will include blind-spots and factors that are hard for most of us to imagine but might have major consequences for clients, professionals, firms, communities and, indeed, society as a whole.

We invite you to explore futures that might unfold in relation to AI and associated developments such as big data, data access, regulation and ethics, with a particular focus on the implications for mid-market law and accounting firms in the UK. While our focus has not been on COVID-19 or health generally, the emergence of the global pandemic as we developed these scenarios prompted us to check our assessment of the uncertainties faced by mid-sized law and accounting firms in the UK. We suggest that you use these scenarios not to re-imagine a post-COVID-19 world – which is being done with varying degrees of effectiveness by others – but rather to think broadly about the extent to which your organisation is equipped to respond to new unknowns. Leaders of professional services firms must ask themselves four fundamental questions:

1. What could the future landscape for professional services look and feel like?

2. What are the potential opportunities and implications of AI for clients, the accounting and legal sectors, and our business?

3. How do we best prepare for the medium and longer term?

4. How can we leverage new technologies such as AI to retain a competitive edge?

Moreover, professional bodies must ask themselves how they can best support their members and how they might themselves adapt. Policymakers and regulators must ask themselves to what extent their current roles and ongoing activities will result in better economic and social outcomes for the sectors they oversee and regulate, and what forms of oversight and intervention they might themselves anticipate. Such thinking about the future is also an opportunity to use insights and resources not fully engaged in firefighting; to re-tune the business; and to attend now to the longer term. Questions include: Which critical assumptions about your business landscape have become invalid, or even toxic? Which new uncertainties have arisen? Which elements of your current strategy, culture, business model, client portfolio and services need to be adjusted for a world in which we will continue to face high levels of turbulence, uncertainty and ambiguity – especially in relation to issues such as climate change, technology developments and consumer behaviour, as well as economic growth and the ongoing pandemic? How can you ensure that your strategy remains robust and coherent? To what extent is your organisation able to anticipate and respond to this level of ongoing change? Reliance on singular forecasts often leads to bad decisions which tend to be expensive and time-consuming. Assumptions are implicit in our choices, which often makes us blind to the true impact of change and to weaknesses in our strategies. Instead, embracing uncertainty through identifying the drivers of change allows us to develop multiple views of the future. This allows weak assumptions to surface, and adjustments to be made that enable strategies to deliver in multiple arenas. It may appear to involve more work. Yet, if a longer view is taken, the increased probability of a good decision is likely to repay the up-front investment.

4.1.1 Why use scenarios?

Scenarios are plausible, challenging and relevant narratives of future contexts in which the user may find themselves. They are not predictions, preferences or forecasts. Scenarios are most helpful when considered as a set, usually two to four possible futures, not a single future. One cannot expect any given scenario to 'come true' as it stands. Rather, using scenarios is intended to help you learn and generate insights, both from exploring each scenario individually and from comparing and contrasting them.

Scenarios are created for a specific user, use and purpose. They are like maps of places no-one has visited yet. There are no photos, reports, or data sources from that future place. Instead, visual charts, maps and stories help us navigate through the uncertainty. In the early 1970s Shell imagined a scenario in which oil-producing countries would organise themselves. As a result, it was better prepared for the emergence of OPEC than its competitors. Good scenarios are rigorously constructed to address the most critical questions that decision makers face. They are most useful when they lie at the edge of what is considered plausible.

Most users find the biggest benefit of scenarios is that they allow for difficult conversations to take place in a safe environment, namely in imagined futures. In respect to our scenarios, we propose these outcomes:

- **For leaders:** Using scenarios can help you focus your thinking, sharpen your strategies and make better decisions.

- **For policymakers and regulators:** Using scenarios can help you gain a better understanding of potential futures for a key group of firms in the UK's largest business sector.

- **For professional bodies:** Using scenarios can help identify how best to support members.

Image: RF Studio on Pexels

4.1.2 How we developed these scenarios

To build stories of the landscape for professional services firms in 2030, we adopted the scenarios approach associated with the Oxford Scenarios Programme.[69] The project team first conducted desk research and interviews with stakeholders and firms to identify factors that affect our everyday lives but cannot easily be influenced or changed by any single firm. This 'contextual environment' includes the political landscape, legislation and environmental and demographic change. These factors in turn affect the 'transactional environment', which has a more immediate impact on our work as professionals and includes our interactions with, for example, employees, clients, competitors and regulators. After establishing a broad contextual and environmental framework, the factors most likely to influence the sector in 2030 were identified. Through extensive debate and discussion with professional services firms and stakeholders, including a workshop with 30 expert participants in summer 2019, the team then generated the building blocks for the scenarios.

69 Ramirez and Wilkinson, 2016; Ramirez et al, 2010

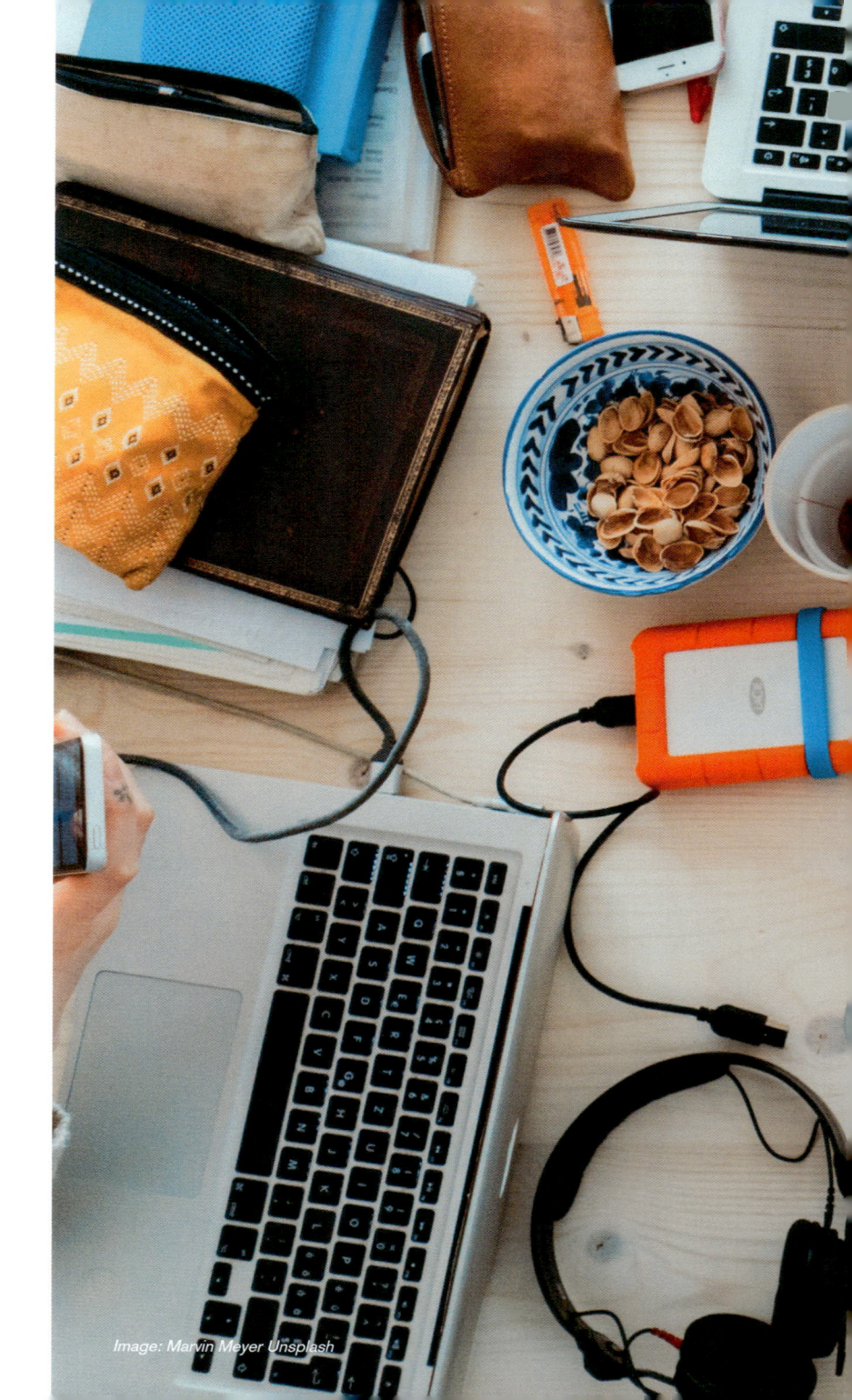

Image: Marvin Meyer Unsplash

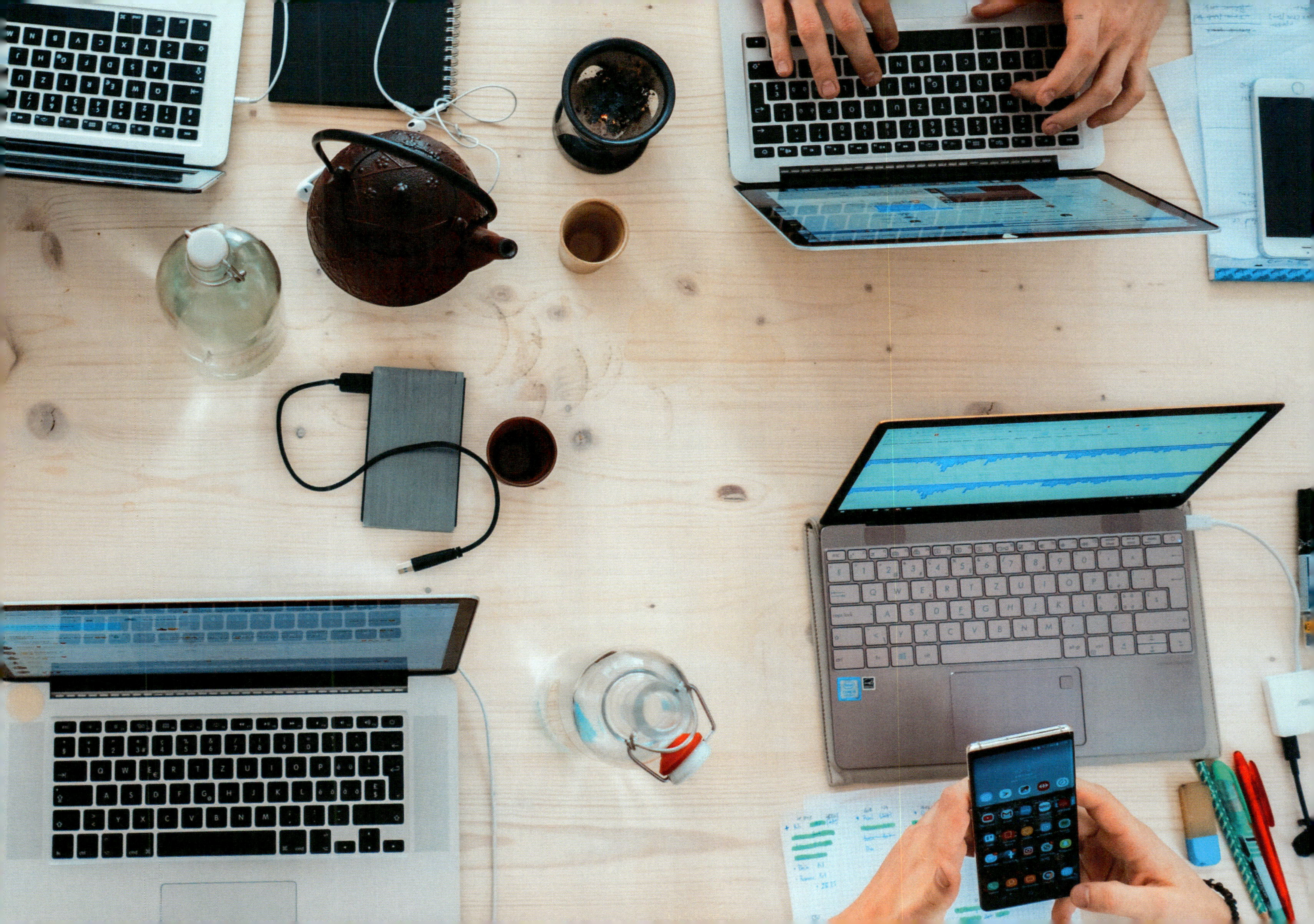

4.2 Overview of the 2030 scenarios

We produced three equally plausible 2030 scenarios. In each scenario, structural and technological changes evolve and interact in different ways, leading to different outcomes. In summary, these are worlds where professional services look quite different:

1. Platform Domination
A small number of very large firms and networks access private 'data lakes' to provide a wide range of services across borders and jurisdictions. Small and mid-size firms survive in niches.

2. Bumpy Superhighway
New entrants with digital and data skills provide AI-based non-protected services, with reduced prices and increased quality – benefitting from new models, deep pockets, existing strong brands and positive attitudes towards long-term investment. All incumbents struggle.

3. Value Kaleidoscope
Clients use AI-enabled search across a wide range of suppliers, underpinned by the same regulated AI. Full-service firms lose their advantage, providing many more opportunities for small and mid-size firms. However, pricing pressures lead to reduced profitability for all.

4.2.1 Using scenarios to convert insights into action

Scenarios serve as a valuable tool for:
- Strategic decision-taking. Evaluate the resilience and vulnerability of different options regarding specific strategic decisions (for example, a business development option or large investment).
- Strategy evaluation. Evaluate the viability of an existing strategy and identify any need for modifications and/or contingency plans.
- Strategy development. Develop a strategy that is robust enough to deal with the wide variations in business conditions across all the scenarios.

Image: JR Korpa on Unsplash

4.2.2 Using scenarios to help with organisational learning

Scenarios provide leaders with the ability to:

- Enhance a strategy's robustness by identifying and challenging underlying assumptions and established wisdom
- Make better strategic decisions by discovering and framing uncertainties, leading to a more informed understanding of the risks involved with substantial and irreversible commitments, and contributing to strong and pre-emptive organizational positioning
- Improve awareness of change by shedding light on the complex interplay of underlying drivers and critical uncertainties, and enhancing sensitivity to weak and early signals of significant changes ahead
- Increase preparedness and agility for coping with the unexpected by making it possible to visualise possible futures and mentally rehearse responses
- Facilitate mutual understanding and collaborative action by providing different stakeholders with common languages and concepts in a non-threatening context, thereby opening the space for creating robust, effective and innovative multi-stakeholder strategic options.

4.2.3 Building an anticipatory capacity in the firm

When firms create their own scenarios they often choose to revisit their set of scenarios periodically, so they remain relevant and challenging. Others have a development cycle. Shell, for example, generates scenarios over several years and then uses them across the organisation for a period of time before restarting the process. During a crisis, events unfold rapidly and the sense of time feels compacted.

However, this means that plausibility can be stretched. Some organisations draft scenarios for closer futures and have to be prepared to change or replace them more quickly. Others establish a scanning capacity to identify new insights or uncertainties as they emerge, allowing them to adjust the set of scenarios and/or change direction on an ongoing basis.

Image: Anna Shvets on Pexels

4.3 Three scenarios for 2030

Platform Domination
Illustration: Kat Hassan

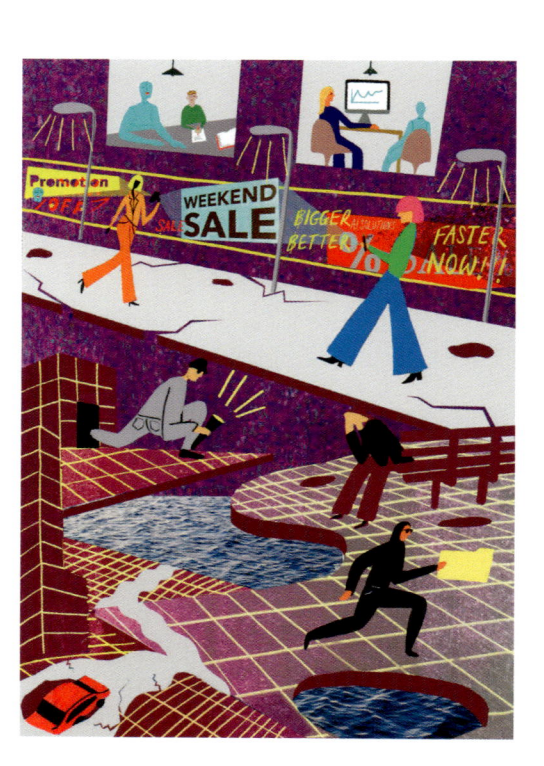

Bumpy Superhighway.
Illustration: Kat Hassan

Value Kaleidoscope.
Illustration: Kat Hassan

Here are some suggestions for leadership team discussions in relation to each of the three 2030 scenarios that follow:

Using these scenarios to stage strategic conversations can help organisations prepare now for the only certainty we have; that the future is unknown and unknowable.

- **For each scenario ask: "If this scenario was definitely going to unfold, how well do we think our firm would perform?"**

- **For each scenario ask: "If this scenario was definitely going to unfold, does our firm have the right AI and related capabilities to be successful?"**

- **"Is there anything that our firm is doing right now that would not work at all in WHATEVER scenario we end up in?"**

- **"Is there anything that our firm could do (or is doing already) that would work very well in ANY of the three scenarios?"**

4.3.1 Scenario comparison table

	Platform Domination	**Bumpy Superhighway**	**Value Kaleidoscope**
A world where...	A few 'platform' businesses control access to data infrastructures, setting the rules for everyone else including those needing access to data to train algorithms or automate services.	People are surrounded and targeted by ever-updating, personalised, surveillance-based digital services underpinned by invisible and minimally regulated automated data-sharing and analysis – with uneven outcomes for business and for society.	AI is integral to connecting, monitoring, evaluating and auditing organisations and individuals allowing them to achieve business goals aligned with stakeholder value, which is increasingly tied to positive environmental, health and social impacts.
Professional services industry structure	There are fewer, larger firms, resulting from consolidation. Small and mid-size firms survive in niches.	Consolidation between law, accounting and other professional services in response to new entrants including tech players.	Specialisation and in-depth expertise are valued. Professional advice is more affordable.
Standing of the professions	AI-enabled professional services using large datasets result in fewer errors and greater consistency.	AI-augmented advisory and audit services are tied to collaborative professional expertise, rather than individual professions.	Specialisation and in-depth expertise are valued. Professional advice is more affordable.
Divergence between law and accounting	Differences between law and accounting matter less. The Big Four extend their footprint in law, building on expertise in analysing large data and standardised procedures.	With a shared focus on solving client problems, and access to combined business datasets and AI tools, differences between professions matter less.	Regional mid-sized firms combine local knowledge and networks, with AI-enabled analysis.
Future professionals and their work	New career opportunities have emerged but there are fewer jobs outside the dominant players.	New entrants offer new ways of working, attracting qualified professionals and others with related skills.	Millennials exercise their values in clients and professional services. Emphasis on individual lifelong learning, not building up firms.

	Platform Domination	**Bumpy Superhighway**	**Value Kaleidoscope**
UK economy, politics, standing and trading environment	A more assertive EU; restrictions on trade in products and services with UK. UK imposes restrictions on inward/outbound trade, travel and active border management, except with key partners.	UK offers a low regulation, pro-investment environment. International firms, including tech giants and Chinese investors, are free to operate in the UK.	Emerging multi-nation alignment and cross-border regulation on sustainable growth. Strong UK policy emphasis and investment on levelling up.
Global trading and economic environment	Low growth, with supply chains organised within distinct geo-political trade blocs. A federal EU with several markets with strong protections. Limited international collaboration around regulation and data-sharing – resulting in the 'splinternet'.	Low or medium growth, but very uneven. Tech giants in partnership with local players push digitalisation and datafication into many sectors.	Low growth, with reduced supply chains involving China. Confident EU. New levels of co-ordination and regulation among global actors and regional actors. 'Value' reframed, tied to addressing pandemics, carbon, water and food.
Technology diffusion	Competing standards set by the dominant platforms. Little innovation. Devices and software are rarely truly global.	Much innovation but quality varies as does consumer safety. Cybersecurity is a new big issue and opportunity.	Certified code is monitored and assessed by government.
Societal acceptance of AI	Acceptance of targeted, personalised, media-rich digital experiences underpinned by AI. Democrats and activists worried by surveillance and political messaging.	Wide acceptance of automated services. AI is embedded in the everyday for consumers, but on a patchy basis.	Increased surveillance is acceptable for shared social, health and environmental goals.
Regulation and oversight	The big platforms control and charge for access to data for national security and risk management and have significant lobbying power.	Multiple and inconsistent frameworks and guidelines.	AI platforms, data access, 'black boxes' and markets are highly regulated at international and national levels.
Data access and management	Big platform businesses control and charge for access to centralised data lakes. Small firms risk fraud and fines from using bootleg data.	A new breed of data warehouse providers manages and stores data and provides services.	A shift from data privacy to data sharing for health and social goals.

2030 scenario comparisons.

4.4 Scenario 1: Platform Domination

This is a world where a few 'platform' businesses control and charge for access to data infrastructures, setting the rules for everyone else.

About this world

In 2030, a small number of very large firms – with 'platform' business models – have access to private 'data lakes' used to deliver and customise services across borders and jurisdictions. AI is now invisible and routine, built into many products and services, including the dark web, underpinned by strong regulation. Consumers trust platform firms, but democrats and activists are worried by surveillance and political messaging.

Professional services

AI-enabled professional services firms pay for access to the data lakes, resulting in fewer errors and greater consistency and reliability. This increases the standing of top tier professionals. Small and mid-size professional services firms survive in niches, sometimes creating risks for themselves and clients by using bootleg data, resulting in fraud and fines. Profits are thin and innovation is limited. In this world, big platform firms – some with origins in technology, while others are conglomerates with expertise in data management and analysis – control and charge for access to centralised data lakes nationally, regionally and globally. In 2030, small and mid-sized firms do not have the resources to join up data 'pools' into data lakes. Sharing of data across markets or borders and jurisdictions is now more complicated and an additional cost of doing business.

By the end of the decade, in professional services there are a few dominant firms, with very few firms at the mid-market level. The important differences between professional firms are not about traditional expertise, but size and range of work. Once text data became analysable in the same way as numerical data, the firms with expertise in large scale data analysis, including large accounting firms, began to apply these techniques to law. Mid-decade, the Big Four extended their footprint in legal services, building on their expertise in standardised procedures and acquiring frontier firms across the professions. But in 2030 there is a competitive advantage for large law firms, who can now get value from their own and clients' textual and other data, compared to small law firms.

By the end of the decade, a few big, elite, full-service professional services firms serve the big platforms, with integrated data management. Large firms own or can access private 'data lakes' (often including what used to be called 'public' data) to provide a wide range of services across borders and jurisdictions, leveraging their networks of professionals working with clients in different countries, with access to data lakes used to train algorithms, and deep knowledge of changing issues in industry sectors. Small and mid-size firms survive in niches, especially based on common law and areas of business that are hard to automate. AI-enabled professional services using large datasets result in fewer errors and greater consistency and reliability, increasing the standing of top tier professionals. Profits are thin and innovation is limited. Fees have declined because of intensity of competition.

Automation of routine tasks, reduced travel, AI adoption and new societal priorities as a result of pandemics removed drudgery from professional services work, allowing for greater focus on what really matters to clients and professionals. Face-to-face relationships with clients matter, for those willing to pay for such access to professionals. But what really matters is access to data, algorithms trained across large data lakes and the associated know-how. New career opportunities for the workforce have emerged but there are fewer jobs outside the dominant players. Despite a loud 'social mobility' agenda in large firms, diversity among staff remains low, except where clients demand it to meet their own environmental, social and governance objectives. Top tier firm networks serving the platform businesses and global elite attract talent. Small firms in niches invest in building and retaining specialist expertise, but profit sharing and progression are limited.

From the perspective of society as a whole, in the UK in 2030 there is social acceptance of targeted, personalised, media-rich digital experiences underpinned by AI and digital surveillance. AI is now invisible and routine, built into many products and services, including the dark web, resulting in more crime as well as positive outcomes for society. Consumers trust the big platform firms, and brands built upon them, who have clear responsibility and liability

Platform Domination. Illustration: Kat Hassan

in relation to AI. Bias is acknowledged by the platforms with efforts to minimise it, but the reality is that, as data oligopolies, the platforms define what bias is and what to do about it. Democrats and activists are worried by the resulting discrimination, surveillance and political messaging. Consumers are unaware of the trade-offs being made in terms of privacy and their own human agency when they access AI-enabled services, with little face-to-face contact with customer service agents, colleagues or peers. People still value face-to-face interactions with professionals, but these are high cost. Universal Basic Income is widely available, supporting a disenfranchised class without meaningful work.

Years of low economic growth and political upheaval after COVID-19 led to the emergence of calcified geo-political trade blocs: EU, North America, China, Russia, and their allies and spheres of influence. They have different and often incompatible approaches to growth and managing challenges such as virus outbreaks, border restrictions and security. Within these blocs, supply chains are highly integrated; across them, trade in goods and services, data sharing and investment are limited and sometimes highly regulated. International collaboration is limited, with the blocs advancing competing approaches to regulation and data-sharing, resulting in the 'splinternet'. Within blocs, however, there is good access to data-driven, real time products and services delivering personalised experiences across multiple devices, tied to platform businesses and their data.

During the previous decade, sufficient EU member states pushed for Europe to function as a federal, innovation-friendly platform and single market, with strong protections in place. In the post-COVID-19, post-Brexit settlement, this more assertive EU imposed restrictions on trade in products and services with the UK, which also introduced restrictions on inbound and outbound trade, travel and active border management, except with the US. In 2030, UK professionals have to get certified to operate in the EU and internationally; EU standards are the norm. UK businesses with international markets found themselves consolidating inside one or more geo-political blocs. Starting new business relationships was hard to achieve, remotely. Often, the EU was the easy choice with existing clients or networks in place.

During the second half of the decade, regulation of AI came to be organised in mutually exclusive silos. The big platforms control and charge for access to data for national security and risk management and have significant lobbying power. Closed standards, formats and certified technologies are controlled by the dominant platforms, supported by regulators to exclude external players from their markets. Devices and software are rarely truly global because the hand-offs across jurisdictions in terms of regulation and security are complex and expensive to manage. As a result, a very few platform businesses have global access to data and markets, negotiated across these geo-political blocs. Only very large professional services firms, organised in networks, can invest in supporting their clients to achieve compliance with regulations and standards across all the blocs. Small professional firms using bootleg data and tools to cut costs face problems and fines from errors and fraud.

Things to look out for between now and 2030:
- The formation of large, monopolistic businesses controlling and charging other businesses and governments for access to data
- Competition and other regulatory authorities becoming less powerful
- Closed standards emerging, controlled and certified by a few players, which are inconsistent across borders
- Large law firms routinely analysing their own and client data with new tools
- Big accountancy firms expanding into legal services.

Winners in this world:
- Big professional services firms (and networks of firms), able to access and use large datasets
- Consumers able to access media-saturated, experience-rich targeted services
- Businesses and professionals with capabilities in data management, integration, security and analysis, a core requirement in this world.

Losers in this world:
- Businesses without access to their own and customers' data
- Small and medium-sized professional services firms
- Citizens concerned about unequal access to products and services
- Traditional professional services firm employees.

Interview with a retiring professional, 2030

Janet Preece founded Preece+Co with two colleagues in 2002 when she was in her mid 30s. She built the business up over time from being a general practice law firm to one that is specialised in high volume consumer law – flight delays in particular have provided a large chunk of 'bread and butter'. Janet has always been keen on technology, much more so than most lawyers. She gets this from her dad, who worked for Acorn computers back in the early 1980s before PCs came to dominate. She remembers his drive for technological excellence. But being the best isn't always a winning strategy. Her dad used to tell the story of how Bill Gates visited little Acorn and was impressed by how much more sophisticated their operating system was than MS DOS but Gates went on to be the world's richest person while Acorn went bust. She studied biology at university, only later converting to the law.

Preece+Co have been at the forefront of applying technology to law. The first big change came when the Covid pandemic happened a decade ago. The firm was able to shift quickly and profitably to online delivery. Her interest in technology ramped up and she saw new opportunities. Janet remembers how they worked with Manchester University's computer scientists in Star Trek t-shirts to apply artificial intelligence to decision making. For example, with flight delays you want to know will the airline accept the claim is valid, or will they fight, and if they fight what are your chances of winning. If you can eliminate the cases that the airline will fight and win then your success rate soars and you don't waste money on loosing cases – it is a 'no win no fee business' after all. In fact, that was just the beginning, because identifying winning and losing cases did not require artificial intelligence in the form of machine learning at all – it just required coded data and regressions. Later, machine learning was applied which improved the predictions.

In those days law firms competed against each other on the basis of their services. This included price competition. By focusing on high volume cases Preece+Co could also get by with very few qualified lawyers. They preferred paralegals – qualified lawyers not only expect to be paid well, but expect to be fed interesting work, and that was not in abundant supply. Paralegals were just the ticket.

Then the government and the insurance industry changed the award rates on personal injury compensation almost overnight which destroyed a good chunk of their business.

Back then, the government still essentially set the rules. But over the last ten years there has been huge consolidation in professional services. The big professional services firms with their deep pockets already had access to lots of client and business data. It was one step to consolidate that and combine it with travel firm data, and they were able to limit access to the data to anyone who did not want to meet their terms.

Looking back upon her career in the law, she says the core training in assessing evidence and making judgements has served her well. Preece+Co gave her and her co-founders a good living, and provided a good living to their employees and their dependents; in total, hundreds of people in Handforth in South Manchester, not a place full of opportunity.

But when her son John mused that he would like to follow her into the law, she was both proud and horrified. Just as she could not have followed her father into the computer business and enjoyed the same success, nor could John now do what she has done – times have changed. Just as Microsoft's dominance killed off Acorn, now the Big Three's domination in professional services has killed off opportunities for mid-sized independent law firms. He might try to become a dentist, she mused – that still pays well and has resisted automation. Or he might follow his grandfather in computers – at the interface of computers and human intelligence. That, surely, will be in demand for the foreseeable future.

4.5 Scenario 2: Bumpy Superhighway

This is a world where people are surrounded and targeted by continuously updated, personalised, surveillance-based digital services, underpinned by invisible and minimally regulated automated data-sharing and analysis – with very uneven outcomes for business and for society.

About this world

In a push for economic growth after the COVID-19 recession, the UK government allowed tech giants in partnership with local players to push digitalisation and datafication into many sectors. As a result, in 2030 AI is embedded in the everyday for consumers and for business, but on a patchy basis. The speed at which this happened led to regulatory gaps and missed opportunities to make AI algorithms and data access safe, fair and explainable. Cybersecurity is a new big public policy issue, a business concern with insider and external threats, and dedicated professional specialism. The information superhighway appears to have been realised, but with bumps, potholes and limited oversight.

Professional services

Following the opening up of professional services sectors in the early part of the decade, new entrants launched AI-based, non-protected services, benefitting from new business models, deep pockets, strong brands and positive attitudes towards long-term investment. All incumbent professional services firms struggled, leading to consolidation. In 2030, clients benefit from reduced prices and increased quality for professional services. But quality varies, as does consumer safety.

The world of 2030 sees low to medium economic growth, driven by tech-enabled innovations in several sectors including healthcare, retail and education, but with uneven gains for consumers and uneasiness in civil society. Post-COVID-19, in a push for economic growth, the UK government and regulators allowed tech giants in partnership with local players to push digitalisation and datafication into many sectors. Policy makers in the EU and US also stepped back from significant regulation, in particular regarding trade in products and services, AI and foreign direct investment. In 2030, AI is embedded in the everyday for consumers and businesses, but on a patchy basis depending on the sector, and rarely signposted as such. Convenience and price matter more than privacy concerns.

From the point of view of consumers, in 2030 there is now wide social acceptance of automated services in health, travel, retail, high end social care and public services. With new and prolonged pandemics, such services enable adaptation to temporary lockdowns, limited travel and social distancing rules. There's openness to new forms of working, connecting with colleagues and families, and uses of data. However, managing data privacy, liability for errors related to AI and addressing AI-enabled discrimination is piecemeal, so while there is acceptance of AI, it's context-specific.

Multiple digital and data formats, standards and norms came into being over the decade, alongside an active dark AI web. Diffused, wide scale gathering and sharing of data is routine in business and the public sector. But there are numerous overlapping standards and formats resulting in confusion, short-termism and illegal practices. As a result of the variability of data governance practices, and failures of the criminal justice system and lawmakers to act in response to serious organisational failures, service quality varies, as does consumer safety. Trust is easily lost with safety and data breaches. In the early part of the decade, as working at home became normalised because of COVID-19, this introduced new security issues to businesses. There is heightened data vandalism, crime and terrorism. Each time there is a significant cybersecurity event, regulators play catch up on data, AI and digital but then drop the issue. In response to this opportunity, a new breed of cybersecurity professional has emerged.

In 2030, EU/UK relations and trade in products and services continue on the basis of mini-agreements. UK professional qualifications are recognised in the EU, so UK professional firms can find opportunities there. But there are tensions within Europe, which to some eyes has crumbled from a Brussels monolith to a two-speed Europe with local adaptation by member states on some regulations. Doing business there requires a willingness to navigate the sometimes inconsistent rules across European member states.

Bumpy Superhighway. Illustration: Kat Hassan

Image: Fauxels on Pexels

In the early part of the decade, some professional services firms were able to adapt rapidly post-COVID-19, including accounting firms winding up failed businesses, law firms supporting M&A following COVID-19 business failures, and reviews of policy mistakes. But then the government opened up previously protected areas of professional services work. International firms, including tech giants and Chinese-owned organisations, were now free to operate in UK professional services. New entrants launched AI-based, non-protected services, benefitting from new business models, deep pockets, strong brands and positive attitudes towards long-term investment. More flexible subscription models and on-demand services were offered by new entrants. At the end of the decade, audit is built into standard business software. Consumer legal services such as wills are built into social media platforms, which already have detailed information about people and their networks. Regulations and compliance are built into smart devices.

Clients benefit from reduced prices and increased quality for professional services. But quality varies, as does consumer safety. By mid-decade there was consolidation among incumbents of all sizes to cope with the threat of new entrants. Over the decade accountancy firms in particular seized the opportunity to build on their expertise in analysing client data to expand into enabling digital transformation. Small firms remained strong in niches but had to develop new forms of expertise in working with clients and their data. In 2030 there are more one-stop-shop firms, with integrated professional and data expertise, able to support clients to understand and respond to changes in their industries.

These days, professional standing is linked to the contributions to achieving societal outcomes in health, environment and security that professionals can demonstrate. But this expertise is now ordinarily understood as AI-augmented, rather than being tied to individual, specific professions, or traditional skills. The differences between law, accounting and other professional services matter less than they used to, and standards and skills vary widely. In 2030, what matters is solving client problems by having reliable access to business datasets and AI tools. The new breed of tech-enabled professional services firms attracts young talent to the workforce, as well as qualified lawyers and accountants and those from other areas such as data analytics. By the end of the decade, young professionals routinely look for opportunities outside of traditional firms, which struggled to attract and retain talent. Professional bodies face a crisis of relevance as new firms, types of role, requirements for certification and formats for recruitment emerged.

Managing, acquiring and securing data is now central to any professional services firm. A new breed of data warehouse providers emerge who manage and store data and provide services such as AI and machine learning driven data analysis. International supply chains in low-income countries intensify to clean up and tag data, introducing unforeseen forms of bias and errors. Data storage is fragmented, which can hinder the process of training AI algorithms. Variety in data quality from offshore or data management is an explicit business risk for any client firm.

Things to look out for between now and 2030:
- Major data leak at big UK business impacting significantly on its customers
- Government opening up previously protected areas of law and accounting to new entrants
- Large consumer tech firms building automated audit functionality in business software, with certified professionals providing oversight and additional services
- Social media firms creating a low-cost optional wills feature based on analysis of user data and networks
- Businesses shifting to using online dispute resolution services, based on analysis of past judgements.

Winners in this world:
- Tech firms with deep pockets and strong data and digital expertise
- Consumers and business clients, who benefit from cheaper legal and audit services
- Criminals and hackers, often ahead of weak or inconsistent policymakers and regulators
- Cybersecurity professionals, with new legitimacy and many opportunities.

Losers in this world:
- Small and medium sized professional services firms without core specialism(s)
- Consumers and civil society, impacted by inconsistent privacy and safety laws
- Professional bodies, losing relevance as new organisations, roles and forms of regulation emerge.

Interview with a retiring professional, 2030

I guess we should have seen it coming really, I mean, looking back all the signs were there. And it wasn't like we weren't thinking about it; far from it. We were thinking about it all the time in partners' meetings and strategy days, especially after things calmed down after the first year of Covid. All of us around that table knew that the advance of technology could not be ignored and was changing not only what we did in-house, but how our services were packaged and sold to a rapidly intelligent client base, constantly demanding more for less.

Reflecting now it is easy to be retrospectively intelligent, but in all honesty, I think we did well to keep going as long as we did; maintaining the level of quality and trust expected of us in the face of margin decline, new business structures, alternative career paths as roles changed around technology integration and the types of people we hired morphed to try to accommodate all of this.

And it wasn't easy to lead a firm through. Being flippant, leadership is never easy! Some service lines were so clearly more suited to AI adoption, so we made what were significant investments to the then partners in those spaces. Were we not brave enough? Possibly. Should we have invested more? Possibly. Would greater collaboration have helped? More than likely. But frankly, it is hard to see how our 'little' practice (and I use that somewhat tongue-in-cheek as one of the previous top 25 players in our market) could have done to prepare for this.

Technology advancement can be a uniquely divisive force; you either 'get it' or you don't. If you don't, you can still be accepting of the inevitability and try to adapt, but that's a long way off the people who can see the potential and have the entrepreneurial skills to run with it. For those that wanted to run, they couldn't shake the baggage of the others and put that dynamic into a devolved decision-making framework that characterises a typical professional services partnership firm…. well, let's just say that it makes sense that it wasn't the sector itself that cracked it.

Whether law, accountancy - real estate, even - people who went into the professions were typically attracted by the subject matter; the foundation of knowledge on which they build their careers opining to help solve problems. And let's be frank – the social status too. Using technology to make work easier and expertise of higher quality made intuitive sense and these were the easier to embrace (although certainly not without their pain points during implementation!). But when the fundamental source of knowledge sits inside a machine, that's a completely different proposition and a jump too far for firms whose leadership has been created through the institutionalised professional cultures and underpinning value set bestowed on them historically by society. Adding a handful of non-traditional types around the boardroom, such as a Chief Technology Officer from outside of the sector, helped to build confidence in our investment decisions, but it was never going to be able to deal with an asteroid hit like this.

Which brings me to another obvious point in hindsight relating to scale. Ten years ago in 2020, the professional services space was dominated the Big Four. Yes, their legal capabilities were still relatively in their infancy, but the acceleration of that capacity was tacit. With average turnover then of circa $40bn, they each had scale that dwarfed the leading global law firms, who were just breaking through the £3bn annual turnover threshold. Looking outside the sector and at that time, it was all about the FAANG-tastic five of Facebook ($60bn), Amazon ($250bn); Apple ($260bn); Netflix ($17bn) and Google (Alphabet) ($150bn). Globalisation was – and is – alive and well and taking new forms after the pandemic. In this context, is it any wonder really that the biggest disrupter to the provision of legal and accountancy services came from outside of the sector? What chance did a successful UK professional services firm with an annual turnover of £47m really have in this race? We were tinkering at the edges; rearranging the deck chairs, if you like.

Personally, I am surprised that the Big Four didn't get there, or that they weren't at least a part of the picture, such as a strategic alliance with, say Microsoft or equivalent, to leverage each others' strengths. Why do I think that didn't happen? My best guesses would be a mixture of a number of factors. Private ownership of the global accountants, not only as partnerships, which has challenges that I've mentioned before, but also when you look at each of the Big Four, they present as one company but are in fact a network; a collection of geographical partnerships. I suspect that eventually they weren't able to leverage the collective assets globally as readily as the multi-national corporations.

I also wonder about the strategic alliances in terms of what the professional services firm brings to the party. If expertise and knowledge has been consumed by machines and technology, with machine learning generating insight – and ergo value – then the professional services firms bring a weight of people that the technology firms are neither used to nor need in terms of the embedded skill sets. What would be in it for them in the long term? The tech firms had the resources, the data, the reach and a completely different regulatory approach – it was basically self-regulation for the most of the 2020s.

But let's avoid a regulatory rabbit hole as it's in the detail and misses a substantive macro point. What really is shocking is that the new market dominance has come from the East. Focussing on FAANG is quite a Western viewpoint and at the same time, we should also have been talking about the likes of Ali Baba, and of course Tencent, who are the market leaders, especially after the growth China was able to achieve in the early 2020s. Complacent? Yes. Arrogant? Probably. Either way, I don't think anyone really believed that the global centre for business support would leave the West.

I'd be lying if I said there wasn't a part of me that is still waiting for it to go wrong; for their values to cause them to become unstuck and the wider public wake up to the realities and concerns that feel very real to me. But for now at least, I'm an old-fashioned minority voice, reminiscing about the good old days I guess …

4.6 Scenario 3: Value Kaleidoscope

AI is integral to connecting, monitoring, evaluating and auditing organisations and individuals allowing them to achieve business goals aligned with stakeholder value, which is increasingly tied to positive environmental, health and social impacts.

About this world

'Value' is being reframed. While economic growth remains a priority, there is growing emphasis on working in parallel towards public value in business and government and among consumers tied to addressing pandemics, carbon emissions and water and food availability. Organisations using AI operate within common rules and standards with strong governance. Regulated AI is now built into products and services, underpinned by global monitoring, compliance and reporting, accessible to small and medium-sized businesses and public services.

Professional services

In 2030, clients routinely identify and engage with potential suppliers and advisors using platforms underpinned by the same regulated AI to assemble teams to meet their needs for professional services. Full-service firms have lost their advantage, and there are more opportunities for small and mid-size firms. There is reduced profitability for all professional services firms. The value-add of professionals is at the forefront of people's minds, in an environment in which clients can easily adjust their requirements and preferences, reconfiguring the kaleidoscope of providers and professionals.

The extended rethink in response to COVID-19 led to a new alignment by 2030 on value, fairness and sustainability. Although this took several years to play out, successive corporate scandals in AI and data leaks on the one hand, and growing activism on climate change, access to food and water and inequalities on the other, resulted in a new political alignment internationally, regionally and in the UK. In 2030, there are new forms of co-ordination and regulation among global and regional actors, including a newly confident EU. Dissenting voices are acknowledged and integrated rather than marginalised and excluded - although powerful pockets of resistance to these new values endure.

Technologies regarded as for innovators only in 2020 became central to identifying risks for governments, public services (in particular healthcare and environmental management) and businesses. In the early part of the decade, massive data breaches and fatal accidents involving autonomous vehicles resulted in growing public scepticism about AI. But by mid-decade, stronger regulation of AI was in place in response to informed public discussion and activism, with new criminal charges for firms using AI that resulted in loss of life, investments in enabling data literacy and certification of AI. In this world, AI is seen as integral to monitoring, evaluating and auditing organisations, governments and individuals to assure compliance. Responsibility and liability for AI are clear. Depending on the application, these rest with software developers, those who trained an algorithm and those who provided the data corpus for the AI.

Over the decade, specialist tech firms remained central to digital transformation in business and society. By the second half of the decade governments required tech firms to work closely with regulators and with partners in the sectors they work with, to implement and comply with new standards. People have got used to checking to see if the products and services they use are built on 'Verified AI' certified code, monitored and assessed by the government, boosting social acceptance. In many business sectors and public services, technology is 'plug and play' based on common standards, frameworks and skills. Processes are in place to identify, acknowledge and address the bias built into AI. This makes it easy for even small and mid-size organisations, without specialist IT management skills or substantial funds to invest, to deploy automation and insight-driven solutions for their customers.

Over the decade, this reorientation to new ways of understanding value was evident in how businesses organised and how people consumed and experienced products and services. Investment in, and recognition of, the importance of places meant that local networks of businesses and people thrived. There are still global firms and brands, but the local and regional are acknowledged and celebrated. While there was significant innovation in some sectors such

Value Kaleidoscope. Illustration: Kat Hassan

Image: Negative Space on Pexels

as retail, health and travel post-COVID-19, especially as firms reduced supply chains involving China, this did not translate to substantial economic growth in the UK. In a context in which growth was being reframed, and levelling up across the UK remained a priority, there was sufficient political capital for governments to invest in people and technologies in places. After COVID-19, there were considerable assets under public ownership across the whole of the UK, resulting in opportunities for local professional services firms resulting from the ongoing levelling up agenda. A new National Care Service, complementing the NHS, also resulted in new opportunities for professional services firms, combining regionally based expertise with analysis of integrated big data. Clients with business in Europe invested in building on their links, once the EU and UK agreed to continue cross-border trade in products and services. Most UK professional qualifications were still recognised in EU member states, which meant that professional services firms could access European markets.

After the first phase of COVID-19, cross-border data-sharing in common formats to quickly identify pandemic hotspots and restrict travel became a priority area for governments to reach agreement on. New international agreements on data-sharing about climate change risks followed in the second half of the decade. This resulted in a shift from asking people to give up privacy for security, to data sharing for public health and environmental goals. In 2030, there are clear rules about who owns data and privacy, for example in the form of sunset clauses (to remove data after a specific amount of time) and widespread public datasets. New laws, guidelines and behavioural nudges resulted in people's personal data stored in their personal devices and business data being accessible to new data-integrator services, tied to narratives about public good. From the mid-2020s, governments and regulators began to play a significant role as guarantors of quality, transparency and interoperability of data and AI, with open standards and clear governance. AI platforms, data access and 'black boxes' such as algorithms became highly regulated at international and national levels.

When accessing professional services in 2030, clients are empowered, and oligopolies have been weakened. By the end of the decade, clients came to routinely identify and engage with potential suppliers and advisors using platforms underpinned by the same regulated AI. Fine-grained differences between expertise are understood and appreciated, and new specialisations and roles have emerged. Professional services activities are now best thought of at task level, rather than in terms of firms. Temporary project teams come together with local knowledge and varied professional expertise to meet client needs, with expectation of sharing or accessing a wide variety of data, supported by relevant frameworks and platforms. Over the years, full service professional firms lost their advantage. This created many more opportunities for small and mid-size firms. Account management matters less in 2030. Fee income fell, leading to reduced profitability for all. Regional mid-sized firms, combining local knowledge and networks, with AI-enabled analysis are particularly suited to the new landscape where people travel less, and place matters more.

Reduced margins were balanced with better quality of life for professionals. There were implications too for professional careers. By the end of the decade, millennials make up the majority of the workforce (including clients). In this world there are greater opportunities to exercise their values (in particular, work-life balance, fairness and clarity of purpose). Professional firms operate responsively; they assemble individuals for projects, rather than training and retaining staff over many years. This brings a new emphasis on lifelong learning and development and ongoing certification. Clients and professional services firms invest in building up skills/supporting attainment in under-represented social groups.

Things to look out for between now and 2030:
- Criminal charges and convictions for data breaches and accidents involving autonomous vehicles and non-compliance with health screening
- Development of 360-degree accounting and audit to manage and report on social, environmental and financial outcomes
- International agreements on data sharing in common formats for health and to address environmental issues
- New rules and certification requirements in data management and governance of AI 'black boxes' for professionals.

Winners in this world:
- Professionals with distinctive expertise, confident they will be found by AI-enabled client search and called on to join project teams
- Professional services firms with local networks and depth of knowledge
- Millennials, whose pro-environment and pro-social values are foregrounded
- Business clients, who benefit from assembling teams of mixed expertise in response to their business needs and reduced costs.

Losers in this world:
- Large and full-service professional services firms which have lost their competitive advantage in a world where clients assemble teams of professionals
- Mid-sized professional services firms without a strong location-based focus and relationships and ability to integrate these with digital transformation.

Where do we go from here?
Professionals looking back from 2030

Lawyer: I can still remember a decade ago. The world of law has really changed since then. In early 2020, I was four years into my job, I had worked as a paralegal and junior lawyer, we'd never heard of Covid and the climate emergency was something on the news but not yet catastrophic. I must confess I was about to quit the profession because of the monotony of the work and becoming a partner looked so far off.

Accountant: It's funny because I was close to quitting as well. I had six years in a decent sized accountancy firm under my belt, but was not feeling motivated. I am glad my firm decided to look into AI and figured out where things were going. They basically stood back, looked at what they'd learned from the pandemic and saw AI as critical infrastructure. They suggested that I could go into an innovation role and play around with the technology and see how to take forward the firm's strategy, so I jumped on the idea. I had no idea how to code. It wasn't about coding. But I had to work out what the tech could do for the business and to help our clients adapt for the future.

Lawyer: At the time, I had a young family and I just couldn't give them any time. It was either years of slog waiting to become a partner, or join one of the big firms and see my family even less. I still don't know how I survived those years. Hours and hours marking up contracts, not enough time to really think about the crucial issues and work out effective solutions.

Accountant: Sometimes, you just have to take a chance. I had a family and we were not sure about this new role. But they had seen me toil for long hours and when I told them that I am planning to take this chance, it's a new role, no defined career path, I didn't know what my future will be in the firm but I need something different, they were very supportive. Since then, new regulations have come in, new technology has come in, and I must say I am glad that I made that decision. Every one of the small specialist firms that now deliver professional advice needs an accounting technologist. I'm thinking soon I will be able to set up my own firm.

Lawyer: I am just glad all the changes broke down the barriers. Today I work with lawyers, accountants, technologists and people from other firms when providing service to a client. This was unheard of ten years ago. I have learnt so much by working to solve all the issues associated with a client matter. New graduates are so lucky. I just wonder how much I could have learnt all those years I was just reviewing documents if I had the technology we have now. We were often wary of collaboration and couldn't help clients when the issues went beyond our narrow skillset and experience.

Accountant: I know, for us, now that everything is cloud based, when I tell young entrants or students at universities about how we used to work with different systems, trying to get data in, signing off paper files, they just look at me as if I am telling them fairy tales. They can't imagine a world without the AI we purchase off the shelf and the click and play ability to immediately use the data the client provides.

Image: Scott Graham on Unsplash

Lawyer: To be honest, modern technology has surprised me. I mean a decade ago, we used to wonder if technology would be good enough to deal with precedent-based law, and how it would be regulated. But now when I see technology and how it's regulated, I think we are heading in right direction. Those big firms developing AI can't just do what they want, there are tests and standards.

Accountant: Same here. I remember when I moved into this new role many of my colleagues were worried that if technology came in and started doing everything, what would we do? Or they thought technology couldn't help with the complex things we were doing. They didn't have the ability to imagine how working with AI could change the kinds of things we do for our clients. Or how doing compliance might be associated with things that people really cared about And how it could stop us wasting time on mundane stuff. Of course, for us accountants, clients were also an issue. Some of them were so far behind in terms of technology, and it was a constant challenge to convince them to adopt this new technology. Even after the pandemic some of them still didn't see the need to invest. But now that it has become so easy to adopt new tech, clients can provide the data we need straight away. I am glad how things have worked out.

Lawyer: One thing that was right back then was the belief that structured data is key if AI is to be used. It just took us a while to work out how to regulate the collection of that data. The collapse of the big firms who hoarded data and then suffered leaks helped, I guess. Now things are much more democratic – everyone can access data, kids learn about data literacy at school. But also we all know the rules of the game and how regulators expect data to be handled.

Afterword

Afterword by Astrid Ayel

A professional services firm, like any other business, must continuously adapt to keep relevant to its client needs and prepare for the future to stay competitive. The promise of leapfrogging is popular, but the difficulty is often where to start. This is especially true for firms seeking to understand the potential of AI and how best to embed it within their long-term strategic goals.

The benefits of using and adopting AI and data technologies goes beyond creating efficiencies and improving the practice of professions. The greatest potential lies in re-imagining the firm's business model to truly build future resilience.

This toolkit provides an invaluable fast track methodology to embark on that journey. It is the result of two years of collaborative work between leading academics and industry experts dissecting AI through the lens of a professional services firm. It combines academic formulas of research with pragmatic business approaches and specific use cases. It includes all steps necessary to achieve a successful outcome starting with a collaborative approach to innovation.

This particularly resonates with the objectives of AI for Services, a network established by KTN and funded by UKRI bringing together leading professionals, academics and high growth entrepreneurs researching and developing innovative solutions, to share learnings, discuss common challenges and further encourage innovation transfer. The diversity of its members demonstrates that AI has become a multi-disciplinary field that integrates social and behavioural science. Its application to professional services perfectly sits at the intersection of humans and machines. The future for professionals could not be more exciting.

Astrid Ayel
AI for Services Lead
KTN

References, credits & acknowledgements

References, credits & acknowledgements

References 178
Credits & acknowledgements 183

References

Agrawal, A., Gans, J. and Goldfarb, A. (2019). *Economic policy for artificial intelligence. Innovation Policy and The Economy*, 19, NBER Books series, pp 139-159.

Alarie, B., Niblett, A. and Yoon A. H. (2018). How artificial intelligence will affect the practice of law. *University of Toronto Law Journal*, 68, pp 106-124.

Aletras, N., Ash, E., Barrett, L., Chen, D., Meyers, A., Preoţiuc-Pietro, D., Rosenberg, D., and Stent, A. (2019). *Proceedings of the Natural Legal Language Processing Workshop*. Stroudsberg, PA: Association of Computational Linguistics.

Aletras, N., Tsarapatsanis, D., Preoţiuc-Pietro, D., and Lampos, V. (2016). Predicting judicial decisions of the European Court of Human Rights: A natural language processing perspective. *PeerJ Computer Science*, 2, e93.

Amoore, L. (2020). *Cloud Ethics: Algorithms and the Attributes of Ourselves and Others*. Durham: Duke University Press.

B2C2 v Quoine (2019). *Singapore International Commercial Court SGHC(I) 03*. [ONLINE] Available at: https://www.sicc.gov.sg/docs/default-source/modules-document/judgments/b2c2-ltd-v-quoine-pte-ltd.pdf [Accessed 15 December 2020].

Bicchieri, C. (2005). *The Grammar of Society: The Nature and Dynamics of Social Norms*. Cambridge: Cambridge University Press.

Björklund, T., Maula, H., Soule S. A. and Maula, J. (2020). Integrating design into organizations: The coevolution of design capabilities. *California Management Review*. 62 (2) pp 100-124.

Brinckmann, J., Grichnik, D. and Kapsa, D. (2010). Should entrepreneurs plan or just storm the castle? A meta-analysis on contextual factors impacting the business planning-performance relationship in small firms. *Journal of Business Venturing*. 25, pp 24-40.

Brooks, C., Vorley, T., Gherhes, C. and Capener, J. (2018a). *Innovation in the Professional Services Sector*. [ONLINE] Available at: www.emits.group.shef.ac.uk/blog/wp-content/uploads/2018/05/Report-Innovation-in-the-professional-services-sector.pdf [Accessed 9 November 2020].

Brooks, C., Gherhes, C. and Vorley, T. (2018b). The nature of publicly funded innovation and implications for regional growth: Reflections from the Sheffield City Region. *Competitiveness Review: An International Business Journal*, 28(1), pp 6-21.

Brooks, C., Gherhes, C. and Vorley, T. (2020). Artificial intelligence in the legal sector: Pressures and challenges of transformation. *Cambridge Journal of Regions, Economy and Society*, 13 (1), pp 135-152.

Brown, T. (2009). *Change by Design: How design thinking transforms organizations and inspires innovation*. New York: Harper Collins.

Brydon, D. (2019). *Assess, Assure and Inform: Improving audit quality and effectiveness. Report of the Independent Review into the quality and effectiveness of audit*. [ONLINE] Available at: assets.publishing.service.gov.uk/government/uploads/system/uploads/attachment_data/file/852960/brydon-review-final-report.pdf [Accessed 26 November 2020].

Buchanan, B. (2020) *The AI Triad and What It Means for National Security Strategy*. Washington, DC: Center for Security and Emerging Technology.

Casadesus-Masanell, R. and Zhu, F. (2013). Business model innovation and competitive imitation: The case of sponsor-based business models. *Strategic Management Journal*, 34 (4), pp 464-482.

Competition and Markets Authority (2016). *Legal services: Making it easier for consumers to choose a lawyer*. [ONLINE] Available at: www.gov.uk/government/publications/legal-services-cma-recommendations/legal-services-making-it-easier-for-consumers-to-choose-a-lawyer [Accessed 26 November 2020].

Cohen, M.A. (2018). Law Is a Profession and an Industry - It Should Be Regulated That Way. *Forbes Magazine*. [ONLINE] Available at: www.forbes.com/sites/markcohen1/2018/03/29/law-is-a-profession-and-an-industry-it-should-be-regulated-that-way/ [Accessed 9 November 2020].

Curle, D. (2017). *Alternative Legal Service Providers: Changing Buyer Perception.* [ONLINE] Available at: blogs.thomsonreuters.com/answerson/alternative-legal-service-providers-buyer-perception/ [Accessed 9 November 2020].

Dang, T.K. (2019). AI transforming the world. *Forbes Magazine.* [ONLINE] Available at: www.forbes.com/sites/cognitiveworld/2019/02/24/ai-transforming-the-world/ [Accessed 9 November 2020].

Faulconbridge, J. R. and Muzio, D. (2017). Global professional service firms and institutionalization. In Seabrooke, L. and Henriksen, L. F. (Eds) *Professional Networks in Transnational Governance.* Cambridge: Cambridge University Press.

Financial Reporting Council (2018). *Key Facts and Trends in the Accountancy Profession.* [ONLINE] Available at: www.frc.org.uk/getattachment/27725654-8bd9-4623-a410-ef1661a69649/Key-Facts-and-Trends-2018.pdf [Accessed 9 November 2020].

Girotra, K. and Netessine, S. (2014). Four Paths to Business Model Innovation. *Harvard Business Review.* [ONLINE] Available at: hbr.org/2014/07/four-paths-to-business-model-innovation [Accessed 26 November 2020].

Gray, D., Brown, S. and Macanufo, J. (2010). *Gamestorming: A Playbook for Innovators, Rulebreakers, and Changemakers.* Sebastopol, CA: O'Reilly Media.

Greenleaf, G., Mowbray, A. and Chung, P. (2018). Building sustainable free legal advisory systems: Experiences from the history of AI and law. *Computer Law & Security Review*, 34, pp 314-326.

Herbert Smith Freehills (2017). Artificial intelligence: The client perspective. [ONLINE] Available at: www.herbertsmithfreehills.com/latest-thinking/artificial-intelligence-the-client-perspective [Accessed 23 November 2020].

Hoshino, N. (2019). *Retailing in an Era Without Online/Offline Boundaries – Japan's Path To OMO.* Tokyo: Mitsui & Co. [ONLINE] Available at: www.mitsui.com/mgssi/en/report/detail/__icsFiles/afieldfile/2020/01/07/1911i_hoshino_e.pdf [Accessed 18 December 2020].

House of Lords (2018). *AI in the UK: Ready, willing and able?* Select Committee on Artificial Intelligence. Report of Session 2017-2019, HL Paper 100. [ONLINE] Available at: publications.parliament.uk/pa/ld201719/ldselect/ldai/100/100.pdf [Accessed 9 November 2020].

ICAEW (2018). *Artificial Intelligence and the Future of Accountancy.* [ONLINE] Available at: www.icaew.com/technical/technology/artificial-intelligence/artificial-intelligence-the-future-of-accountancy [Accessed 23 November 2020].

IRN Research (2019). *UK Legal Services Market Report (9th Edition).* [ONLINE] Available at: www.irn-research.com/market-research-reports [Accessed 26 November 2020].

Kingman, J. (2018). *Independent Review of the Financial Reporting Council.* [ONLINE] Available at: assets.publishing.service.gov.uk/government/uploads/system/uploads/attachment_data/file/767387/frc-independent-review-final-report.pdf [Accessed 26 November 2020].

Katz, D. M. (2012). Quantitative legal prediction-or-how I learned to stop worrying and start preparing for the data-driven future of the legal services industry. *Emory Law Journal*, 62, pp 909-966.

Keeley, L., Pikkel, R., Quinn, B. and Walters, H. (2013). *Ten Types of Innovation: The Discipline of Building Breakthroughs.* London: Wiley.

Kimbell, L. (n.d.). Methods. [ONLINE] Available at: serviceinnovationhandbook.org/methods/ [Accessed 17 December 2020].

Knapp, J., Zeratsky, J., and Kowitz, B. (2016). *Sprint: How to Solve Big Problems and Test New Ideas in Just Five Days.* London: Bantam Press.

Kokina, J. and Davenport, T. H. (2017). The Emergence of Artificial Intelligence: How Automation is Changing Auditing. *Journal of Emerging Technologies in Accounting*, 14 (1), pp 115-122.

LawGeex (2019). *Legal Tech Buyer's Guide 2019.* [ONLINE] Available at: ltbg2019.lawgeex.com/

Law Society, The (2018a). *Artificial Intelligence and the Legal Profession: Horizon Scanning Report*. [ONLINE] Available at: www.lawsociety.org.uk/topics/research/ai-artificial-intelligence-and-the-legal-profession [Accessed 9 November 2020].

Law Society, The (2018b). *Six ways the legal sector is using AI right now*. [ONLINE] Available at: www.lawsociety.org.uk/news/stories/six-ways the-legal-sector-is-using-ai/ [Accessed 23 November 2020].

Legal Services Act (2007). [ONLINE] Available at: www.legislation.gov.uk/ukpga/2007/29/contents [Accessed 26 November 2020].

LexisNexis (2014). *Workflow and Productivity in the Legal Industry*. [ONLINE] Available at: www.legaltechnology.com/wp-content/uploads/2014/11/Legal-Professional-Efficiency_whitepaper_final.pdf [Accessed 9 November 2020].

Liedtka, J. (2020). Putting technology in its place: Design thinking's social technology at work. *California Management Review*, 62 (2), pp 53-83.

McAfee, A. and Brynjolfsson, E. (2012). Data Scientist: The Sexiest Job of the 21st Century. *Harvard Business Review*. [ONLINE] Available at: hbr.org/2012/10/data-scientist-the-sexiest-job-of-the-21st-century [Accessed 26 November 2020].

McCarthy, J. (2007). *What is artificial intelligence?* [ONLINE] Available at: http://jmc.stanford.edu/articles/whatisai/whatisai.pdf [Accessed 9 November 2020].

Magretta, J. (2002). Why business models matter. *Harvard Business Review*. [ONLINE] Available at: hbr.org/2002/05/why-business-models-matter [Accessed 9 November 2020].

National Academies of Sciences, Engineering, and Medicine (2018). *Data Matters: Ethics, Data, and International Research Collaboration in a Changing World*. Washington, DC: The National Academies Press.

Osiyevskyy, O., Hayes, L., Krueger, N. and Madill, C.M. (2013). Planning to grow? Exploring the effect of business planning on the growth of small and medium enterprises (SMEs). *Entrepreneurial Practice Review*, 2 (4), pp 36-56.

Osterwalder, A., Pigneur, Y., and Tucci, C. L. (2005). Clarifying business models: Origins, present, and future of the concept. *Communications of the Association for Information Systems*. [ONLINE] Available at: aisel.aisnet.org/cais/vol16/iss1/1/ [Accessed 26 November 2020].

Ovaska-Few, S. (2017). How artificial intelligence is changing accounting. *Journal of Accountancy*, October 10. [ONLINE] Available at: www.journalofaccountancy.com/newsletters/2017/oct/artificial-intelligence-changing-accounting.html [Accessed 23 November 2020].

Oxford Economics (2018). *The Accountancy Profession in the UK and Republic of Ireland: A Report for the Consultative Committee of Accountancy Bodies*. [ONLINE] Available at: www.ccab.org.uk/wp-content/uploads/2020/06/The-Accountancy-Profession-in-the-UK-and-Ireland.pdf [Accessed 9 November 2020].

Ramírez, R., Selsky, J.W., and van der Heijden, K. (2010). *Business Planning for Turbulent Times: New Methods for Applying Scenarios, 2nd ed.* London: Earthscan.

Ramírez, R. and Wilkinson, A. (2016). *Strategic Reframing: The Oxford Scenario Planning Approach*. Oxford: OUP.

Ribstein, L. (2010). The death of big law. *Wisconsin Law Review*, 3, pp 749815.

Rostain, T. (2017). Robots Versus Lawyers: A User-Centered Approach. *Georgetown Journal of Legal Ethics*, 30, pp 559-574.

Scott, W. R. (2008). Lords of the dance: Professionals as institutional agents. *Organization Studies*, 29, pp 219-238.

Smith, C. M. and Shaw, D. (2019). The characteristics of problem structuring methods: A literature review. *European Journal of Operational Research*, 274 (2), pp 403-416.

Slaughter and May (2017). *Superhuman Resources: Responsible deployment of AI in business*. [ONLINE] Available at: www.slaughterandmay.com/media/2536419/ai-white-paper-superhuman-resources.pdf [Accessed 9 November 2020].

Spiegelhalter, D. (2019). *The Art of Statistics: Learning from Data*. London: Penguin.

Stone, P., Brooks, R., Brynjolfsson, E., Calo, R., Etzioni, O., Hager, G., Hirschberg, J., Kalyanakrishnan, S., Kamar, E., Kraus, S., Leyton-Brown, K., Parkes, D., Press, W., Saxenian, A.,Shah, J. Tambe, M. and Teller, A. (2016). *Artificial Intelligence and Life in 2030: One Hundred Year Study on Artificial Intelligence*. Stanford, CA: Stanford University.

Susskind, R. and Susskind, D. (2015). *The Future of the Professions: How Technology Will Transform the Work of Human Experts*. Oxford: Oxford University Press.

Sutton, S. G., Holt, M. and Arnold, V. (2016). "The reports of my death are greatly exaggerated"—Artificial intelligence research in accounting. *International Journal of Accounting Information Systems*, 22, pp 60-73.

Taran, Y., Boer, H. and Lindgren, P. (2015). A business model innovation typology. *Decision Sciences*, 46, pp 301-331.

Turner, J. (2019). *Robot Rules: Regulating Artificial Intelligence*. London: Palgrave Macmillan.

Zott, C. and Amit, R. (2007). Business model design and the performance of entrepreneurial firms. *Organization Science*, 18, pp 181-199.

Zuboff, S. (2019). *Surveillance Capitalism: The Fight for a Human Future at the New Frontier of Power*. London: Profile Books Ltd.

Image: Dmitrij Paskevic on Unsplash

AI Readiness

Credits and acknowledgements

This toolkit is an output of research funded by the UKRI Industrial Strategy Challenge Fund which took place between 2018-21. The academic partners in the project were (in alphabetical order): Lancaster University, Manchester University, Oxford Brookes University, Sheffield University, and University of the Arts London. The other partners in the project were The Managing Partners' Forum and NormannPartners. While the text is co-authored, some sections draw in particular on academic research by specific authors.

Authors of specific sections

Introduction
Lucy Kimbell, Cristian Gherhes, Ezri Carlebach, Tim Vorley, Hilary Smyth-Allen

Cases and approaches
James Faulconbridge, Martin Spring, Atif Sarwar

Business model innovation
Tim Vorley, Cristian Gherhes

Opportunities and challenges of AI adoption
Cristian Gherhes, Carlo Cordasco, Ezri Carlebach

Future scenarios
Lucy Kimbell, Gerard Drenth, Makayla Lewis, Hilary Smyth-Allen, Bruce Tether, Martin Spring, James Faulconbridge, Richard Chaplin, Tim Vorley

Toolkit methods
Toolkit methods developed by Lucy Kimbell, Makayla Lewis, Cristian Gherhes, Hilary Smyth-Allen, Tim Vorley

Illustrations
2030 scenarios illustrated by Kat Hassan
Design of templates and tools for the methods by Makayla Lewis, Lucy Kimbell, Suky Best

Acknowledgements
Thank you to all the participants in legal and accounting firms and regulators who took part in the design sprints (online and face to face), webinars and workshops we ran during 2018-20. These allowed us to test and refine the design sprint methodology outlined in this book. Thanks also to the project's advisory board who provided insights and perspectives from across the professional services sector. We also acknowledge the support of the funder, UK Research and Innovation, without whom this toolkit would not have been developed, tested and realised. Thank you to Peaks Krafft for input to the discussion on AI and ethics.